CULTURE
SHOCK

A BIBLICAL RESPONSE TO TODAY'S MOST DIVISIVE ISSUES

CHIP INGRAM

BakerBooks

a division of Baker Publishing Group
Grand Rapids, Michigan

© 2014 by Chip Ingram

Published by Baker Books
a division of Baker Publishing Group
P.O. Box 6287, Grand Rapids, MI 49516-6287
www.bakerbooks.com

Printed in the United States of America

Library of Congress Cataloging-in-Publication Data is on file at the Library of Congress, Washington, DC.

ISBN 978-0-8010-1612-7 (cloth)
ISBN 978-0-8010-1660-8 (ITPE)

To protect the privacy of those whose stories have been shared by the author, names and some details have been changed.

Published in association with Yates & Yates, www.yates2.com.

14 15 16 17 18 19 20   7 6 5 4 3 2 1

I dedicate this book to Blythe, Ella, and Emory; Nola, Ryder, and Sam; Miles and Jessie; and last but not least, Noah.

I pray they will hold unswervingly to the truth of Jesus and His Word and communicate that truth by life and word with winsomeness and love.

Holy Father, I ask You to protect these little ones from the spirit of this age and ever-changing winds of what is deemed right and wrong. May they know You deeply and trust You fully. Help them hold unswervingly to the truth that is in Jesus and His Word, even when to do so means to be unpopular or even persecuted. Cause them to see and treat others as You do, Lord Jesus.

Help them to so winsomely and radically love all kinds of people, from all kinds of backgrounds and all kinds of beliefs and all kinds of lifestyles, that Your heart and Your truth would be powerfully revealed through them.

CONTENTS

ACKNOWLEDGMENTS

This book has been in the making for a very long time. I didn't know it at the time, but looking back, it's now obvious. In the mid-1970s, I was a new Christian, unwilling to "throw my brains in the trash" and blindly believe what was so at odds with the spirit of the "make love not war" and "if it feels good, do it" mentality of my era.

As I wrestled with the major tenets of Jesus's teaching, His claim to be God, His claim to be truth, His insistence that His Word and Scripture are truth and authoritative, His teaching on sex, marriage, idols, loving your enemies, and His claims to be the unique and only means of the forgiveness of sins and author of eternal life, I began an intensive journey to examine the evidence.

I have to thank Steve Vogal, who introduced me to Francis Schaeffer as we traveled through South America, playing basketball and sharing Christ. I am forever indebted to the graduate faculty at West Virginia University, who allowed me to write my master's thesis on the philosophical basis of teaching ethics in sports, and in so doing, allowed me to do extensive historical and philosophical research on what and how truth, values, and reality have been determined both inside and outside the Church through the millennia. I am grateful for the requirement to verbally defend my thesis (all three and a half hours) before brilliant professors who forced me to think at a new level and answer every objection imaginable. They challenged the core of my beliefs and the Biblical teaching concerning truth as an absolute, objective, nonchanging reality.

I also want to thank Country Bible Church in Texas, Santa Cruz Bible Church in California, Walk Thru the Bible in Georgia, and Venture Christian Church in Los Gatos, California, for the privilege of helping me work out in real time the application of truth as it applies to these controversial and often divisive issues in both very conservative (rural Texas) and very liberal (Santa Cruz) environments.

God, in His mercy and wisdom, allowed me to minister to, and learn to love rednecks who used racial slurs, leaned far right, and didn't use words like "gay" when referring to those who practice homosexuality. Later I would live and minister in one of the most politically correct cities in America. They viewed the University of California at Berkeley as too far right. I got to know and deeply care about liberal politicians, radical feminists, gays and lesbians, new agers and passionate environmentalists.

As a pastor seeking to teach the same truth that was radical and unpopular with both groups for very different reasons, the pressure to conform in each situation was immense. But the big lesson was how similar both groups and I were with one another. Out of our insecurities, prejudice, and backgrounds, we all held the others with suspicion, assumed the worst, accepted labels, and defended and judged rather than seeking to meet, know, and understand one another as unique individuals.

I've learned a lot in the last thirty years pastoring these very different groups, and then teaching the very same truth in almost one hundred countries with Walk Thru the Bible. The real issues are not abortion, sexuality, homosexuality, politics, or the environment; these are merely the lightning rods of conflict and controversy. The real issue before the Church today is "What is true?" and then "How is that truth communicated?" I'm deeply thankful for the privilege of learning from ultra-conservatives and ultra-liberals. I know from personal experience what truth shared in love can do.

My plea for a strong, clear stand on Biblical truth as absolute and authoritative could not have been more countercultural in Santa Cruz, California; but when we translated that same truth to meeting real needs, driving HIV patients to the doctor or grocery store, addressing poverty and runaway teens, and meeting with gay public officials to address the needs of our city . . . everything changed.

When God's direction was to build relationships with blacks and Hispanics and even move the church into an African American neighborhood in rural Texas, I was extremely unpopular with some, to the say the least. Yet, years later, I watched one of the most adamant objectors, whose vocabulary had been filled with racial slurs, mentor boys from the neighborhood and teach them a craft to earn a living. His heart changed. He loved them and they loved him. When we baptized at the African American church across the street (because we didn't have a baptistery), we helped one another; prejudice and suspicion were replaced with genuine caring relationships.

So, I thank God for letting me watch the power of His truth when shown in love. This isn't a book to bash anyone or build a case for some particular group. The Church is losing its commitment and courage to believe and stand for what Jesus and our forefathers in the faith have given their lives for.

Yes, some have used truth as a club, but today we have become so fearful of appearing unpopular, anti-intellectual, or intolerant that we have become bland, lukewarm, and anemic. We are not **bold** because we don't know what we believe or why. We are not **loving** because we have missed Jesus's heart and His deep compassion for every person regardless of their gender, race, beliefs, or sexual orientation.

So finally, a big thank-you to Jerry and the Living on the Edge team who made this book possible. Thank you, Chad and the Baker Books team, for your support and commitment to me and this project. Thank you, Venture Christian Church, for the privilege to live this out, by God's grace, in the most diverse city in America. Thank you, Curtis and the Yates & Yates team, for your insight and for building the bridges that led to this book. And thank you, Theresa, for being an amazing, patient, loving, and prayerful wife, without whom I could never have done this.

INTRODUCTION

This book is for Christians. It is about issues we don't normally discuss. We often argue about these issues or scream about these issues or say nothing about these issues, but we rarely sit down and have meaningful, deep, respectful conversations around these issues.

These issues polarize! Within the larger Christian community, there are a great variety of views and opinions concerning human sexuality, homosexuality, abortion, the environment, and politics.

These are the kind of issues that bring division and confusion in families, small groups, and churches. As a result, Christians—except for a vocal minority on the opposite sides of these issues—have been strangely silent. Many, if not most, followers of Christ report that they have never heard a message from the pulpit on politics or the environment, let alone human sexuality, homosexuality, or abortion.

The result is a generation of sincere Christ-followers who have embraced the values and morals of our culture rather than those of God's Word, to our own detriment.

This book is written for those of us who take seriously our relationship with Christ, His Word, and His ultimate directive to love God with all our heart, soul, mind, and strength, and our neighbor as ourselves.

We unashamedly believe that the Bible is God's Word, and we have experienced a supernatural, spiritual birth that has radically changed our lives and our eternal destiny. We want to be authentic, grace-filled followers of Jesus, who live out our faith 24/7 and long to be instruments of life and love to those around us.

We are deeply concerned about injustice, famine, and slavery around the world and the ever-increasing violence, moral erosion, and family disintegration here at home.

We are equally concerned and disheartened by two, common vocal responses to the moral and cultural issues of our day.

We cringe with remorse and embarrassment when we hear hate-filled speech and name calling and see violent actions by "Christians" in their effort to address issues like abortion, homosexuality, and the environment. We understand their passion for truth and moral fidelity but perceive their method and lack of love to be anything but Christlike.

On the other end of the continuum, we are equally dismayed by those in the Church who have abandoned or compromised the moral absolutes in Scripture. In the name of tolerance, relevance, political correctness, and compassion, they have embraced popular culture's views on human sexuality, abortion, and homosexuality as "Christian" views while violating the clear teaching of Scripture. We understand their passion to champion God's grace and acceptance, but grace without truth is unloving and—again—anything but Christlike.

This book is an honest effort to get Christians talking openly and respectfully about these issues. It's an effort to seek out what it looks like for us as followers of Christ to bring to the table both grace and truth in dealing with these issues and the people they impact. I've tried to present the presuppositions of both sides of the issues and report research and statistics in context.

I certainly have a bias, but we all do. Most of all, Jesus does, and that's the "bias" I want to get clear on and follow. Jesus brought light, not heat. He confronted unpopular and controversial issues with clarity and truth, but He treated people with dignity and respect unless their motives and hypocrisy dictated otherwise.

For too long the Church has been silent on these issues that are shaping our culture. For too long opposing groups have thrown rocks, slanted statistics, and vilified one another, even within the Church.

Jesus promised that the truth would set us free. Let's explore the truth together. He also commanded us to love one another. Let's put truth and love together and explore what the Bible says about today's most divisive issues.

CHAPTER 1

WHATEVER HAPPENED TO RIGHT AND WRONG?

I am the way and the truth and the life. No one comes to the Father except through me.

John 14:6
Jesus of Nazareth

I f you are old enough, you may remember a time when the difference between right and wrong was clearly understood in America. Even those who committed criminal acts did so in spite of knowing better. Up until the beginning of the last half-century, all of recorded human history had been characterized by a clear understanding of moral absolutes. From the Babylonian Code of Hammurabi to the Judeo-Christian ethic, every culture declared certain behaviors to be wrong and evil.

America's standards for moral behavior and ethics sprang largely from the Ten Commandments, the teachings of Christ, and the letters of the apostle Paul. Regardless of one's political preference, race, or socioeconomic status, society generally had consensus on a number of core values and moral absolutes: the value of human life, loyalty, respect, fidelity, commitment to family and marriage, responsibility, kindness, generosity, forgiveness, and love.

Things have changed, and the symptoms of this change are all around us—in today's paper, on the news, on the internet, in the next cubicle, and likely in your own home. The following article is a distressing one, and I apologize for its graphic nature. But I share it with you because it illustrates an important point. Slowly read this account and ponder carefully the future consequences of this kind of thinking and behavior in our world.

Seventeen-year-old Elizabeth and her fourteen-year-old friend, Jennifer, made the mistake of taking a shortcut that night. It was 11:30 p.m. on a hot, steamy June night, and the two had just left a party at a friend's house. They called home to let their folks know they were on their way, but they never made it. As Elizabeth and Jennifer cut through a wooded area near White Oak Bayou, in Houston, Texas, they stumbled into the initiation night of a gang called Black and White. Gang members had descended on this little area to drink some beer and engage in a macho induction that involved newcomers fist-fighting other members. The gang had just started to break up when the girls came in to sight. "Let's get 'em," one of the gang members cried. Elizabeth and Jennifer's naked bodies were found four days later. They'd been raped repeatedly. Both girls had been strangled—one with a belt, the other with a shoestring. Apparently the girls didn't die quickly enough. According to police experts, evidence showed that both of their necks had been stepped on to complete the executions. Six gang members were charged with the murders. Police reported that all six youth had participated in the rapes and murders, and they ranged from ages 14 to 18.

One of the gang members had appeared on a local television show the day before the murders. He hoisted a beer and boasted into the camera, "Human . . . life . . . means . . . nothing." Basically, that message had reached the core of his being. Human life means nothing. Another of the boys upon hearing that they may be charged with murder is reported to have exclaimed, "Hey! Great! We finally made it to the big time."[1]

What a horrific event. Can you imagine anyone being so calloused, so confused about reality, so incredibly depraved as these young men?

Unfortunately, as we all know, this tragedy is not an isolated case. Moral chaos has permeated our schools, our streets, and often our homes. In fact, in the next twenty-four hours in America, 1,000 unwed teens will become pregnant, 500 adolescents will begin using drugs, and 6 youths will commit suicide. That's not in a year, not in a month . . . that's *every twenty-four hours* in America![2]

Even many of those who should be setting positive examples for younger generations are instead setting the pace for immorality, inventing new ways to "push the envelope" in regard to degrading behavior. It has become commonplace to read of university administrators misusing funds, padding their salaries, and making obscene phone calls from their campus offices. The nightly news is filled with sordid stories about prominent politicians, professional athletes, business leaders, and even clergy who are involved in adultery, drugs, illicit sex, or domestic violence.

What on earth happened? How did we get here? How did we get to the place where young teens boast of killing one another, where schools require security checkpoints, and where young government interns fall prey to lecherous politicians?

The Core Issue

Opinions on this issue are a dime a dozen. Some say we should spend more tax money on education reform, urban development, or family planning clinics. Others say we need to win the war on drugs or build bigger prisons.

But I believe we need to dig deeper and examine what is behind these symptoms and what they tell us about our national moral crisis.

The core issue is that we've lost our foundational understanding of what is right and what is wrong. Our nation—from our leaders to our youngest schoolchildren—has become confused about whose values, ethics, and morals we should adopt as our own. **Values** are core beliefs or desires that guide or motivate attitudes and actions. **Ethics** is the standard of conduct that indicates how one should behave on moral issues arising from principles about right and wrong. Professors, politicians, preachers, and pundits all teach their own brand of ethics.

We've lost our foundational understanding of what is right and what is wrong.

But who is "right" about right and wrong?

This question really boils down to an even more foundational question: **"What is truth?"** We can't know what is right to do in any given situation, or make decisions about education or morality or social behavior until we discover what is true. From the 1950s to today, our nation's understanding of truth has shifted dramatically, so that what was once clear is now clouded with ambiguity and confusion.

In this chapter my goal is to explore the issues, cultural events, and philosophical changes that have brought us to this point. I am going to trace, in a thumbnail sketch, the mountain peaks of our cultural landscape as we look backward through history. Some of the information is somewhat academic in nature, but the implications are incredibly practical.

For those interested in exploring this shift in depth, I've highlighted four books to guide your journey under the heading "Read for Yourself!" I hope you'll take the time to really think through the issues presented. I cannot overstate how absolutely essential it is that we understand not only *why* we are in our current state of moral crisis but also *how* we got here. Each of the following chapters will deal with a specific divisive issue, both inside and outside the Church, but all are dramatically affected by our view of truth.

The Big Question: What Is Truth?

Sixty years ago the answer to the question "What is truth?" would have been relatively easy to find. You could have asked any businessman, homemaker, or student, and they at least would have been able to point you in the right direction. While they might not always have done the "right thing," they probably would have agreed on what the "right thing" was. Courtesy, loyalty, honesty, faithfulness were definitely right. Lying, cheating, stealing were clearly wrong. The Ten Commandments were on target; the Golden Rule was important to follow. But around 1950 a shift in our popular culture's thinking began to occur. Truth, once viewed as clear and absolute, began to be perceived as relative.

I do not want to oversimplify this complex issue, but for the sake of understanding, let's consider two approaches to truth.

Absolute Truth

When I say *absolute truth*, I am referring to something that is always right and true, whether people agree or disagree with it

Read for Yourself!

Four authors are pivotal in illustrating and understanding how the shift from absolute to relative truth occurred. I highly recommend them.

Among Intellectuals—*Mere Christianity* by C. S. Lewis (1952). The famous Oxford professor and atheist-turned-apologist traces his journey and the philosophical basis for moral absolutes, truth, and its implications with regard to faith in God.

In Culture—*The God Who Is There* and *Escape from Reason* by Francis Schaeffer (both 1968). Schaeffer was a Christian theologian and philosopher who accurately anticipated and predicted our current dilemma, tracing the historical and philosophical roots of the shift from absolute to relative truth. His writings had incredible impact in the last quarter of the twentieth century, and the accuracy of his predictions adds greater weight today.

In Education—Allen Bloom, who is not a Christian author, took an extremely critical look at our universities in his book *The Closing of the American Mind* (1987). He pointed out that instead of being a safeguard of what is true, the universities have allowed relative truth to invade every area of academics. Bloom has been a professor at Cornell, Yale, and the University of Chicago, and concluded that as a result of this invasion of relative truth, Americans don't know how to think. Bloom writes, "Because they can't think, they don't know right from wrong, and, unable to make good decisions, they make bad decisions."

In Law and Science—*Reason in the Balance*, written by Berkeley law professor Phillip E. Johnson (1995), emphasizes that ideas and thinking really do matter. Johnson's book takes a hard look at contemporary culture and provides positive, in-depth reading about the issue of relative and absolute truth.

and whether or not it happens to be part of their experience. If something is *black*, it can't be *white* at the same time. If something is *hot*, it can't be *cold* at the same time. If something is *right*, it can't be *wrong* at the same time. This absolute (thesis/antithesis) view of truth is the way people thought until a group of philosophers began to challenge this concept.

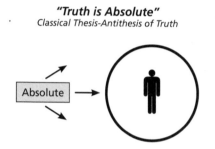

"Truth is Absolute"
Classical Thesis-Antithesis of Truth

In the diagram "Truth is Absolute," the circle represents all of our life experience. The square on the outside represents unchanging truth that is absolute in nature. It affects the realm of experience but is just as true (as indicated by the other arrows) in how it affects all of life, whether experienced or not. An absolute truth in the area of morals and values remains absolute and is true, whether or not you agree with it or experience it.

Think about the earth's gravity for a minute. You may not agree with the theory of gravity, but it remains an absolute just the same. If you step off a three-story building, you will change your belief system very quickly. The reality of the law of gravity does not change. It is an absolute, unchanging truth, apart from one's opinion or experience. When you drop something, even a feather, eventually it will fall to the ground.

The unchanging reality for the Christian is the Word of God; this is the standard for absolute truth. God tells us He is the same yesterday, today, and forever, so we know that His truth cannot be altered simply because we disagree with it.

> **God tells us He is the same yesterday, today, and forever, so we know that His truth cannot be altered simply because we disagree with it.**

In one of the Ten Commandments handed down to Moses, God instructed His people not to murder (see Exod. 20:13). According to absolute truth, murder is wrong. It is not wrong *some* of the time or *most* of the time. Murder is wrong *all* of the time. I think it is safe to say that we all agree that murder is wrong all of the time.

But do you believe that God's absolute truth is just as unchanging when it comes to issues like sexual impurity, lying, stealing, idolatry, and coveting? I think it is safe to say that, as we view the behavior of a great majority of modern Christians, the right and wrong of these behaviors are no longer viewed as absolute.

Relative Truth

By contrast, the second approach considers truth to be *relative*. This concept of truth says life is validated *not* by a set of principles or outside objective data but on the basis of **personal experience**. This is the definition of existentialism, a philosophy that plays out in attitudes and belief systems that say

- If it feels good, do it!

- Do your own thing.

- You choose your truth, I'll choose mine.

- Hey, whatever works for you.

- Who are you to judge me? (the one we've *all* heard before)

Sound familiar? These are phrases heard all too often in America today, and they signal the shift that has been made from absolute to relative truth. Now negotiable truth can be freely altered to suit the person, the mood, or the situation.

"Truth is Relative"
Existential Concept of Truth

If you take a look at the "Truth is Relative" diagram, you'll notice that inside the circle is a little dotted square. This represents truth as the individual perceives it to be through his or her experience. Therefore, truth is different for different people. **It's no longer clear, objective, or consistent—it's just a matter of taste.** You can do your own thing and I'll do mine. We won't judge each other about what is right and what is wrong. To do so would be intolerant.

Actually, it seems as though the only absolute in our culture today is tolerance, which really is contradictory in this context. Those who cry tolerance are themselves intolerant of the people they see as intolerant! What they really mean is, "Agree with me and you won't be intolerant."

How did we arrive at this place where relative truth is so thoroughly embraced? How could something as basic and foundational as our answer to "What is truth?" change so dramatically and so quickly?

CHAPTER 2
HOW DID WE GET INTO THIS MESS?

To the Jews who had believed him, Jesus said, "If you hold to my teaching, you are really my disciples. Then you will know the truth, and the truth will set you free."

John 8:31–32
Jesus of Nazareth

To answer that question I invite you to join me on a brief historical journey. Let's look at the road "truth" has traveled so that we might begin to understand, for example, how a teenager could so brutally take another's life—without remorse or even recognition of wrongdoing.

History Tells the Story

For centuries and centuries the concept of truth, and therefore man's understanding of right and wrong, was by its very nature absolute. Truth came to us from God, by revelation, and man's fundamental question about right and wrong was, "What has God said?"

The Middle Ages

Through the first 1,200 years of the Church, the common man or woman did not have access to the Scriptures, and so people depended on the Church as guardian and dispenser of God's Word. Eventually the line between "the Church" and "the truth" became blurred, until there was no longer a distinction between the two. Unfortunately, the Church could not handle this responsibility and taught a number of things that were contrary to Scripture and extremely harmful. This historical period is referred to as the **Dark** or **Middle Ages** (476–1450).

The Renaissance

Eventually the Middle Ages gave way to the **Renaissance** period (c. 1400–1700). The Renaissance (which means "rebirth") produced a great number of intellectual thinkers who returned to both classic Greek literature and historic Christianity. Many of them began to read the letters of the apostle Paul firsthand, which was a dramatic shift from the past. Through the teaching of the Dark Ages, man had come to be seen as small and insignificant, but out of this new birth emerged a renewed view of the nobility and dignity of humankind. This renewed interest in the Scriptures eventually led to a major conflict in the Church.

The Reformation

In 1517 the **Reformation** period began. It was during this time that a Catholic priest named Martin Luther began to study the original scriptural documents for himself. As Luther read through the books of Romans and Galatians, he discovered that the teachings of the Church were often in direct contradiction to the teachings of the Bible. This ignited a revolution, galvanized by Luther's written challenge (Ninety-Five Theses) to the Church, which ultimately resulted in the basis of moral authority being restored to the Scriptures.

The Enlightenment

The **Enlightenment** or the Age of Reason (c. 1700–1800) followed, which brought yet another intellectual shift, this time toward reason. At its core, the Enlightenment was deeply influenced by philosopher and theologian Thomas Aquinas, who taught that

Chip's Story

I grew up in a home where moral values were absolute. Though my parents were not believers until later in life, they held the values taught to them in their childhood. They were both teachers and consequently at the forefront of the most current trends. Existentialism was working its way into popular culture through our educational institutions, and I was grappling, like most young people, with its implications as we moved through the '60s and early '70s. When I was a young adult I became a Christian. For three and a half years I had a great personal experience with Jesus. I knew my sins were forgiven, I experienced peace, and I was learning God's Word and building relationships with other believers. But every time I had a hard question, my only frame of reference was the situational, relative, experiential truth base. I was finding that I needed something more. I had good parents with solid morals and they had set appropriate boundaries for me, but I began to realize that no one had answered my tough intellectual and philosophical questions as I grew up.

I was introduced to the work of Francis Schaeffer in 1976 by a college basketball teammate, and his books became foundational for me. I read *The God Who Is There* with three-by-five cards and a dictionary in hand because Schaeffer used so many words I didn't understand, such as metaphysics, epistemology, and presuppositions.

Next I read *Escape from Reason*, also by Schaeffer, which explained how this movement toward relative truth has permeated the arts and music. Finally I read *He Is There and He Is Not Silent*, which examined the philosophical underpinnings of Christianity. Again and again Schaeffer helped me to see how it all fit together. This trilogy of books became the basis of my master's thesis at West Virginia University, and I have continued to ponder these things for the past thirty-plus years.

all aspects of a man were fallen (affected by sin) except his intellect. **Man's ability to reason now became the focus.** If given enough time, education, and resources, man can fix the world on his own. German philosopher Immanuel Kant expanded this line of thinking, and with specific application in other arenas by Kierkegaard and Hegel, existentialism gained a foothold. A shift in thinking had begun that would eventually set Biblical truth against man's reason. Though these early philosophers had limited impact on popular culture, the seeds of "human reason" as the ultimate authority had been planted, and man had started down the slippery path of deciding for himself what was right and what was wrong.

> **A shift in thinking had begun that would eventually set Biblical truth against man's reason.**

The Industrial Revolution

In the late 1700s the **Industrial Revolution** was developing, producing some of the greatest inventions that have ever occurred in the history of the world. By now man not only considered logic and reason to be more important than Biblical revelation but was also feeling very self-sufficient. The rapid progress in culture, travel, and standard of living had created an environment of empowerment. Man had things under control. He was at the center of the universe, and he did not need God.

The Evolution of Pragmatism

In this era of self-sufficiency **Charles Darwin** (1809–1882) made his entrance in the historical scene with a book called *The Origin of Species*. Considering the theological implication of evolution, you may be surprised to read that Darwin was a theology student. But back then, the world's leading academic institutions—Harvard, Princeton, Yale, St. Mary's—were all theology schools, training the finest minds. At that time it was believed that we lived in a unified and cohesive universe, and academic disciplines made sense only as they related to God. Theology was considered the "queen" of the sciences, and all other departments, from philosophy and sociology to science and mathematics, were secondary.

When Darwin wrote *The Origin of Species* in 1859, it had little scientific impact or support. Yet it set in motion a paradigm shift that would transform not only the scientific community but popular culture as well. You see, cultural change initially occurs in the minds of society's "thinkers," philosophers, and the intellectually elite. They are the ones who write the books, train the students, and fill the universities. Sometimes it takes fifty to eighty years for the impact from these thinkers to reach the level of the man on the street.

Early on, the paradigm of evolution that resulted from Darwinian thinking affected politics, economics, and history more than it did science. The resulting worldview held that everything evolves. To this idea was added the discoveries of Albert Einstein (1879–1955) and his great mathematical theory of relativity. Contrary to previous thought, Einstein's theory stated that you could actually view and evaluate something from more than one reference point. This theory changed physics and mathematics forever. Although it was not his intent (Einstein never claimed or taught that truth is relative), *relativity* became the buzzword of the twentieth century, just as *evolution* was the buzzword of the nineteenth century. People began to think, "*Everything* is relative."

But more was still to come.

Darwin's thought, along with that of biologist Thomas Huxley (1825–1895) and philosopher Herbert Spencer (1820–1903), fanned the flame of relativism until **John Dewey** (1859–1952) and his writings about **American pragmatism** began to change the focus entirely. Up until the turn of the century the primary question educators, parents, and culture itself had been asking was, "What is right and what is wrong?" But Dewey's influence changed the educational system by declaring that what is right or wrong is not the primary issue. The big question became, "What works?" The pragmatist determines the meaning and truth of all concepts by their practical consequences, so he asks, "What will work?" And later this evolved more specifically to, "What will work for me?"

Man had gradually gone from the absolutes of the Scriptures to an idea that he could shape and define his own reality.

Situational Ethics and Relative Truth

It is at this point that we see the emergence of **situational ethics**, which became an important foundation for future change. I remember, from when I was nine or ten years old, my own mother's frustration with this new school of thought. She worked as a guidance counselor and teacher and was required to attend training sessions in situational ethics. The methodology was to provide students with extreme hypothetical situations to resolve. For instance,

"If someone put a gun to your head and demanded that you do something immoral, would you do it if it saved the lives of five people?" Situational ethics undermined and clouded the issue of whether there is "a right" and "a wrong," because it is a system based on relative moral rules that may be modified in the light of specific situations.

Although no one would deny the reality of difficult moral dilemmas in life when conflicting values are present in a situation, this approach effectively communicated that there was no moral absolute. Our public schools became a laboratory for teaching a form of reasoning and problem solving that would impact our culture more radically and pervasively than anyone could have ever imagined.

Situational ethics undermined and clouded the issue of whether there is "a right" and "a wrong."

By the 1960s the philosophical trend that began early in the twentieth century with the intellectual elite had permeated our culture at every level. Ideas introduced into our seminaries in the '20s, '30s, and '40s bore patient fruit, and by the time we entered the Vietnam War, existentialism had hit street level and the call to "do your own thing," the blatant rejection of absolute truth, launched a revolution. Our society began to cast off moral restraint. Free love and free thinking were the order of the day. "If it feels good, do it!" became the rallying cry. This trend exploded in the '70s, and by the time the '80s arrived, it had spawned a generation of greed. The '90s brought the "Me Generation." "I'm going to do what works for me," said the '90s man or woman. "If it feels good to me and makes me happy, I'll do it, because that's what matters most."

Fast-forward to today. Those kids from the '60s and '70s are now parents and grandparents who raised children with few to no moral absolutes in their lives and with little or no exposure to Biblical truth. The result? Children without a moral rudder who, in some extreme cases, commit violent criminal acts with no apparent sign of regret. What began with intellectuals arguing about the nature of truth, God, and right and wrong has now transformed the worldview of an entire generation. **Our violent, narcissistic, noncommittal, "me first" culture is simply the logical and predictable expression of "truth" as a relative, subjective, unverifiable concept.**

Relative Truth in Action

Now that we've briefly examined how this shift in thinking occurred, we need to look at how existentialism and relative truth play out in our daily lives.

A Snapshot from a Local High School

An article written in a local California high school paper a few years ago illustrates this well. Titling his paper "God," the student author writes:

> There are too many things in Christian dogma that I can't accept, the first of which is the idea of universal truth. Good and evil. I can't rationalize that.
>
> All religion is based on a subjective view of the universe.[1]

I wonder where he got that idea. That's not historically accurate or intellectually consistent, but he doesn't know it.

> My problem is that, in your opinion, God made the universe. In other people's opinions, someone else made it. So, on and on it goes. I do believe that everyone is entitled to their own subjective reality.

This is an example of relative truth.

> I just can't see how one opinion is right, and the rest are wrong.

That's called pluralism, it is the product of existentialism, and it means that all views hold equal value—everyone's right about everything all the time, even if those views contradict one another.

> I believe that all religions are right for particular groups, but there is not one religion that is right for everyone. My god is not a god of love, but a god of reason.
>
> Anything that can be explained with facts and charts seems reasonable to me. I worship the idea that nothing is intangible, that man can explain anything given enough time and given the data. My god is not a person or a being. He is an idea.

The tragedy here is that this young man has expressed an intellectual view that does not correspond with reality. How does he explain falling in love? How does he explain the emotions he has when he longs in loneliness for a relationship that matters? How does he explain our universal quest for meaning and significance? He can't!

> We live in a mechanical universe. Your god doesn't exist here. We don't have any equation for love. You know what happens when you die in a mechanical universe? You rot. No clouds, no angels, no free candy bars.
>
> You rot. I rot. Why do I create such a world? Why do I make this place into a machine functioning on random chance and chaos? Why do I make that? It's for the same reason that you make life into the kingdom of God. It's just my opinion of reality.

This high school student, totally indoctrinated by the culture of the day, has philosophically embraced everything I've covered in this discussion: Truth is relative, reality is whatever I experience it to be, everyone is right, nothing is absolute. The number one virtue is tolerance, and all opinions are not just equal; they are all equally right.

All Christians Believe in Absolute Truth, Right?

Lest you think this high school article represents some rare exception in our day, note pollster George Barna's research among evangelical Christians: **54 percent do not believe in absolute truth.**[2] What we have is a total shift in worldview that impacts how we think, evaluate, decide, and live in every area of our lives. Christians "feel" justified in divorcing a spouse because "it's not working" for them. Believers now live dichotomous lives with no twinge of conscience when they arbitrarily choose to obey some Biblical commands and reject others.

Not long ago I talked with a man who had recently embraced Christ and was growing spiritually in a number of areas. He then casually told me he didn't agree with the "no sex before marriage" part of Scripture and that he didn't want that restriction as part of his Christian experience. The rest, he was eager to add, he found very helpful. In other words, man is the final authority, not God, and thus is justified in accepting or rejecting whatever portion of God's Word he deems appropriate.

Sharing Truth in a Relative World

So, how are we as followers of Christ to live in a culture where all the "rules" have changed? How do we proclaim the absolute truth of the gospel when those around us respond with an enlightened "I'm glad that works for you. Great! But we all have to find our truth in our own way"?

The answer may be less complicated than you think. The key is to gently but consistently help those around us see that they do not practice what they preach. No one can function in a world of relative truth. It simply doesn't work! Although our culture pontificates that all views are equally valid ("No one has the right to say what's true for everyone else"), this is easier said in theory in public than lived out in personal reality. I've found that when push comes to shove, people tend to make decisions based on a very clear and absolute sense of what is right and what is wrong. Phrases like "I'm fighting for my rights" and "That's not fair" are meaningless if truth is indeed relative. Who are we to say what's right or what's fair or what is just? Those concepts assume that somewhere there is a standard that applies to all people. Let me give you a quick illustration from a personal experience.

We can all talk about relative truth as much as we want to, but on a personal level we operate on the basis of absolutes.

A few years back, for twelve years, I lived in a very liberal town, where free thinking and tolerance were highly valued. As a result, a variety of colorful characters were drawn to our downtown mall to play music, congregate with one another, and often ask passersby for money. A few years ago this began to cause significant problems with local retailers, who maintained that the strong number of homeless people and panhandlers was hurting walk-in business.

Around that time I was privileged to have lunch with a local government official who also owned a retail store downtown. We had a fascinating conversation that I really enjoyed. We exchanged brief backgrounds and discussed college experiences and the cultural revolutions we had both taken part in. I found myself respecting his intellectual acumen and passion even though theologically and philosophically we were polar opposites. He was trying his best to make a difference in this world based on all the things he had learned and embraced during his schooling at UC Berkeley—relative truth, pluralism, and tolerance. He protested in the '60s and honestly longed to bring about positive change through his progressive views.

But when the conversation turned to local political issues, I learned that he and several others were proposing an ordinance that would prevent the panhandlers, homeless people, and street musicians from sitting on the sidewalks near the retail stores.

Now, remember, according to the tolerant view he espoused, each person would have a right to sit wherever he chose. Every opinion would be justified, and no one person would have the right to tell others what was right or wrong. Yet he was the leading opponent of the "street people's" right to linger, because their freedom of choice was killing his business.

As I drove back to the church office that day, I realized that we can all talk about relative truth as much as we want to, but on a personal level we operate on the basis of absolutes. It's inescapable. We simply choose where we will draw the line—usually where the actions of others begin to infringe upon our personal space, property, or sense of propriety. As sons and daughters of God, we are called to lovingly and consistently help those around us see their hypocrisy (and our own) and help them rethink their view of truth and their relationship with "The Truth"—even as we constantly rethink and refine our own.

So What about You?

Have you thoughtfully considered what you believe to be "right" and "wrong," and why you believe? Is it because that is how your parents believed? Or is it purposely the opposite of what your parents believed? Have you allowed the values you see on television to become your values by default? Maybe you just go along with the logic of your best friend because he or she is smart and successful and seems to have an answer for everything. Or have you unconsciously given up in the midst of the confusion and chosen to take the path of least resistance?

Unfortunately, statistics show that many who consider themselves Christians have compromised their thinking to embrace moral relativism without even realizing it. George Barna and coauthor Mark Hatch reported in their book *Boiling Point* that although 85 percent of all adults claim to believe in God and state that religious faith is very important in their lives, just 1 in 4 adults and only 1 teenager in 10 believes in absolute moral truth. Less than half of those who describe themselves as "born-again" believe that anything is "absolutely true."[3]

> God has spoken clearly and compassionately about what is right and what is wrong for the protection and care of those He loves.

Barna and Hatch went on to make a number of rather startling observations and stated that "the Church is rotting from the inside out, crippled by abiblical theology."[4] Traditional values have been increasingly abandoned as our culture has moved toward moral relativism—individual self-centeredness that is revealed through a focus on independence, personal happiness, instant gratification, tolerance, personal comfort, and the right to make choices that serve one's self-interest above the interest of others. The authors also observed that, unfortunately, Americans often place these factors at the top of the list when looking for a church to attend.

Again, what do you think? What is your view of truth? What we've learned is that how we think about truth makes all the difference in the world. We tend to forget that God has the copyright on what is true. He has spoken clearly and compassionately about what is right and what is wrong for the protection and care of those He loves.

I invite you to explore with me what the Bible says about human sexuality, homosexuality, abortion, the environment, and politics.

CHAPTER 3
HUMAN SEXUALITY
THE TRUTH ABOUT SEX

You have heard that it was said, "You shall not commit adultery." But I tell you that anyone who looks at a woman lustfully has already committed adultery with her in his heart.

Matthew 5:27–28
Jesus of Nazareth

T he speed takes your breath away! Never in the history of the world has a culture and its values concerning sexuality shifted as fast or as drastically as they have in America in the last fifty years. I'm not saying there hasn't been immorality far worse or equivalent to America's in other parts of the world, but never before has a view of sexuality in a nation moved as fast and as far in as short a passage of time. Fifty years ago we were a nation we would hardly recognize today.

In this chapter I want to chronicle this radical shift in our understanding and perspective of sex and reveal the truth about human sexuality.

The Shift

Here are some revealing statistics about the shift.[1] In the 1950s about 5 percent of girls and about 10 percent of boys in high

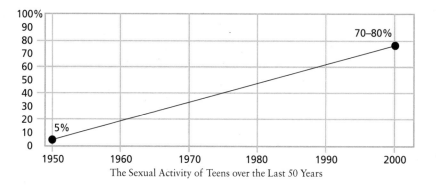

The Sexual Activity of Teens over the Last 50 Years

school were sexually active. Fast-forward five decades and as many as 70 percent of girls and 80 percent of boys are sexually active during high school. Today, 50 percent of all women under thirty cohabitate prior to marriage. The divorce rate in the middle of the twentieth century was in the single digits. Today it hovers around 50 percent. These rapid changes in behavior didn't just happen in general society; they have also occurred in the Church.

In 1969 we shifted into the "no-fault divorce" gear of cultural change. Longstanding legal protections of marriage were being run over or ignored. By 1996 evangelical Christians' divorce rate was 4 percent higher than the national average. All of this has resulted in the stunning shift inside the Church regarding sexuality, marriage, and family.

The statistics that track the speed of change are staggering. For example, in 1987, 75 million people rented a XXX porn video. Five years later, that number had rocketed to 490 million rentals of the most graphic porn. By 1996, the rentals reached 665 million. Pornography is being produced around the world, but the center of consumption is here in America. We distribute more than anyone else.

Recent estimates note that at least 150 new XXX porn videos are created each week. Once the internet exploded they stopped counting rentals. The hidden nature of these activities makes precise figures hard to come by, but about 40 percent of men in America visit porn sites regularly. And the percentage of women who do is increasing rapidly. Not long ago I had a conversation with a friend who is a sex therapist, and she said, "For the first twenty-five years I had no women in my sexual counseling. Now 30 percent of all the people I see for sexual addictions are women."

The numbers I've just mentioned are overwhelming and are often reported a bit higher or lower depending on the metrics used in the studies. My point here is very simple: we have witnessed a dramatic shift in our culture. Like the frog in the water-filled pan on the stove, we finally realize we're in a boiling environment and may feel helpless to get out.

This is when we begin to see signs of the "If you can't beat them, join them" approach invading the Church. I read an article in *WORLD* magazine describing a panel discussion at a Bible conference about sexuality and the Church. One of the participants, a professor from an evangelical school, seemed to be proposing a dangerous form of compromise. It was as if she was saying, "It's fine in church to stand up and talk about God's ideal for sexuality in marriage and all the rest, but the fact of the matter is we know people in their twenties and early thirties are not going to be sexually celibate. So, at the church what we need to do is say, 'Yes, there is an ideal but we need to provide contraceptives in Bible churches so when people disobey the damage will be a little bit less.'"[2]

Now think about that thought process. In other words, the Spirit of God living in Christians no longer has the power to help us obey God, so let's violate one command so maybe we won't mess up on another one.

The Causes

This shift in our view of sex is dramatic. How did it happen?

The shift from absolute to relative truth, the search for freedom in the '60s and the '70s, and bad teaching or lack of teaching in the Church created a perfect storm of consequences. We've done a terrible job. Even people growing up in the Church might have never heard a message on what the Bible teaches about sex.

Add to all that the historical fact that some of our heroes of the faith—Calvin and Martin Luther, to name a few—had a warped view of sexuality. For all they did to bring the Church back to faithfulness to Scripture, they dropped the ball when it came to the Bible's teaching on sex. Martin Luther taught that the only reason for sex, even in marriage, was to procreate. When he stopped being a monk and got married, he had a lot of kids.

> **Silence not only created ignorance and distortion; it set up future generations to be unprepared for the devastating wave of sexual license that followed.**

During the first part of the twentieth century, the Church was still laboring under the distorted picture of a Victorian, snobbish, "sex is dirty and bad" approach to sexuality. The unspoken rule was that you didn't say *anything* about sex. Children, seeing how their parents were uncomfortable, concluded, "Well, sex must be bad, or maybe God is anti-sex." Silence not only created ignorance and distortion; it set up future generations to be unprepared for the devastating wave of sexual license that followed.

Then sexual moral standards changed faster than ever before.

The Impact

The rapid expansion of media and its proliferation into every part of life created a powerful vehicle for advertising. Once the moral floodgates opened, Fifth Avenue realized early on that sex sells. You want to sell toothpaste, cars, or beer? Package them in a subtle or overt sexual setting. Sales will soar! Now we are bombarded in ways that require constant vigilance. Type in the wrong search word on the internet and your computer screen may deliver a moral disaster.

In the face of all this change, the Church has been spiritually impotent. When Christians are obviously exhibiting the same behaviors the world is promoting, the invitation to join us at church or to consider believing in Jesus falls on deaf ears. When our lives are not noticeably different before the watching world, we have little to say even if they decide to pay attention. And why should they? They look at Christians and say, "You're no different than me."

I didn't grow up as a Christian. As a skeptical young adult, I saw the panorama of how the Church mishandled both the problems and the cleanup of sexual misconduct and concluded the Church was hypocritical and irrelevant. I fortunately was introduced to a group of sincere and godly Christ-followers who lived the life and pointed me to Jesus and His Word rather than organized religion. In recent years, however, the sex scandals among televangelists, high-profile pastors, and the public shame of priests' sexual abuse of children have left the reputation of the Church in shambles, leaving our youth more confused than ever and often without anyone in the Church they feel they can trust.

The Cost

The sexual revolution has resulted in over a million people divorcing every year, which leaves one million kids without a stable home. Mom is here, Dad is there, and the family is fractured. Many surviving families display dysfunctions like never before. Unwed teens having babies—children raising children—often alone and compounding the problems.

I will just mention the expanding array of clues that something is going terribly wrong in America: the dramatic rise of AIDS, herpes, incurable gonorrhea, and other sexually transmitted diseases has been staggering in the last forty years. The cost spiritually is the Church's reputation, how the body of Christ is viewed. But even if I were a non-Christian economist, I would have to say the most destructive cost in America the last fifty to sixty years is the loss of our sexual morals. We have spent billions and billions of dollars to help unwed mothers and to support a corrupt welfare system with no measurable improvement. We've invested millions of dollars in various sex education programs and in the prevention of STDs, only to see the behaviors we were trying to prevent actually increase! There is an even more costly day of reckoning coming unless some radical action stems the tide.

Myths and Lies

All this bad news ought to at least cause us to sit down for a while and think about where we are and where we should be when it comes to human sexuality.

You are a sexual being and so am I. How you think about sex impacts your identity, your view of God, and your relationship with others. I'm suggesting that you have been fed lies about sexuality most of your life, regardless of your race, age, gender, marital status, or socioeconomic background.

In fact, I want us to look together at the top six lies or myths you've been fed. Lies are most convincing when they are repeated often enough that they are assumed to be true. This is how lies become myths that we believe. Let's look at these myths, summarize the truth, and talk about how God's truth explodes those myths.

> **Lies are most convincing when they are repeated often enough that they are assumed to be true.**

■ **MYTH 1: God is anti-sex.**

■ **TRUTH: God is so pro-sex He designed it to provide . . .**

- Physical pleasure (Gen. 1:26–27)

- Procreation (Gen. 1:27)

- Relational intimacy (Gen. 2:18–24)

- Spiritual object lessons (Eph. 5:31–32)

The first myth you have been fed is that God is anti-sex. In other words, when sex happens, God goes, "Oh, Gabriel, let's look the other way. Woo!" In this view, sexuality was an accidental side effect in humans that surprised God even more than it surprises us—and He doesn't like it!

The truth of the matter is that God is definitely pro-sex. He created it. He invented sex to provide procreation but also physical pleasure and relational intimacy, and to be a spiritual object lesson of Christ and the church. Sex was no accident; it's in the original design.

God is definitely pro-sex.

The survival of the species depends on sex, but God meant it for so much more! The first two chapters of the book of Genesis give us parallel accounts of creation. In Genesis 1:26–27 we read about God's decision to create mankind.

> **Then God said, "Let us make mankind in our image, in our likeness, so that they may rule over the fish in the sea and the birds in the sky, over the livestock and all the wild animals, and over all the creatures that move along the ground."**
>
> **So God created mankind in his own image,**
> **in the image of God he created them;**
> **male and female he created them.**

Not long after their creation God spoke to them: "God blessed them and said to them, 'Be fruitful and increase in number; fill the earth and subdue it'" (1:28).

Beginning in Genesis 2:7, God provides a detailed account of the crown of His creation and His purpose in the gift of making us sexual beings: "**The Lord God formed the man from the dust of the ground and breathed into his nostrils the breath of life, and the man became a living being**" (Gen. 2:7). Then He replicated that image of Himself by taking a rib from Adam and using it to fashion Eve (vv. 21–23). Except this creature was a little different—the first human female! For Adam, it was love at first sight. When God is the designer and ultimate matchmaker, a couple is bound to connect!

It's at this point that God gave the new couple their wedding blessing: be fruitful and multiply. Translation: the first thing God said to our original parents was, "Make love. Enjoy yourselves. Have babies!" Can I be a little more graphic? "Have sex!"

You don't get fruitful, you don't multiply, unless you have sex! It's holy. It's sacred. God's for it. He created that first couple's bodies like He designed ours. He designed a man and woman to come together in a monogamous, marital relationship. That's God's heart's desire. He looks on the marriage bed as holy, as pure, as a gift, as sacred. He wants sexual experience to be deeply pleasurable.

And then to ensure that procreation happens, God designed us with sexual attraction and desires to make sex happen. But not all sex leads to pregnancy, which brings us to God's rationale for putting Adam to sleep and creating someone who matched him. "The LORD God said, 'It is not good for the man to be alone. I will make a helper suitable for him'" (Gen. 2:18). In God's original design, it's not good for a person to be alone.

God does give the gift of singleness to certain people, and they have a unique set of desires to serve Him in ways that require them to be celibate and single. But for most of us, that yearning in our hearts for connection and attraction to the opposite sex involves marriage. It is in marriage that our God-given desire to be known intimately and to know is fulfilled.

These attractions are more than simply sexual. We want to be known, loved, and connected intellectually, spiritually, emotionally, and psychologically, as well as physically. So in the original wedding ceremony, conducted by the Creator Himself, the brief sermon to the couple informed them that marriage was not only about not being alone but also about creating a new relationship. A relationship that would demand our life partner becomes our number one priority. "That is why a man leaves his father and mother and is united to his wife, and they become one flesh. Adam and Eve were both naked, and they felt no shame" (Gen. 2:24–25). Adam and Eve were naked and unashamed but not just physically. They were emotionally transparent. They were psychologically transparent. They were one with each other and their Creator.

Sex is an awesome, holy, sacred, magnificent gift for our good and to reveal God's glory.

In the Hebrew, the Old Testament uses three words for *sex*. One means "to lie with," another "to go into," and the third "to know." When the Bible refers to David having intercourse with Bathsheba (2 Sam. 11:4), when a man goes to a prostitute, and when sex isn't sanctioned by God, the Bible uses phrases like "they lie together" or "he goes into her" to describe the act. And yet when God's Word describes Adam and Eve's sexual relationship, it says that Adam "knew" Eve. Far from some lustful act for them, sex was about intimacy, connection, and the most intimate kind of knowing. Intercourse was about self-revealing; it was the climax physically of what they were sharing emotionally, intellectually, and spiritually.

Adam and Eve reveal God's design. It's His design for you. Sex is an awesome, holy, sacred, magnificent gift for our good and to reveal God's glory. God is absolutely not anti-sex.

■ MYTH 2: Christians' sex lives and views of sex are dull, boring, and "out of touch."

■ TRUTH: The Scriptures command God's people to be downright erotic in their marital love.

The second myth we must explode is this idea that the sexual lives and views of Christians are dull, boring, and "out of touch." Unfortunately, a lot of Christians have managed to promote this false view of God's gift of sexuality. I grew up with ignorance. I don't think I saw my mom and dad kiss more than two or three times. I didn't observe much overt affection, and neither one sat down and explained God's view of sexuality to me. The biology of sex came to me through public schools and the goal of having sex I learned in the boys' locker room in junior high school.

Later, when I came to Christ, since I'd never heard any healthy, Biblical teaching on sex, I assumed it was taboo. Like my parents, my early Christian leaders simply never addressed the issue, except to say sex was "wrong before marriage." I figured if people really became Christians, they became so holy that sex was a necessary fact of life, like hygiene habits people don't talk about, but my hormones, the media, and culture were screaming, "If it feels good, do it!" I had no clue what it could be like to be a Christian in a God-honoring, gloriously sexy marriage. I don't think I would have had an answer if someone had asked me what Christian couples do in bed.

Growing up as a non-Christian, a lot of my confusion was understandable. I was getting my sexual training in the worst of places. But imagine my surprise to discover, after counseling scores of couples, how many Christians, especially women, have grown up in an environment of silence or distortion about sex. Despite a positive shift in the last ten to fifteen years with some good teaching on the subject, many Christians have major issues with sex in their marriage. They struggle to overcome that sense of sex being "something wrong and dirty" instead of a beautiful gift from God.

> **Scriptures command God's people to be downright *erotic* in their marital love.**

The truth is that the Scriptures command God's people to be downright *erotic* in their marital love. The Bible is not at all awkward about its promotion of a healthy sex life in marriage. Robust sexuality is not merely suggested or casually mentioned as a nice idea. God is pro-sex. He created sex for the reasons defined. Inside of marriage, He commands us, literally, to be erotic. To deeply enjoy one another and relish giving pleasure to our mate for life.

Listen to Solomon, the wisest man on the earth, as he counsels his son. "May your fountain be blessed, and may you rejoice in the wife of your youth. A loving doe, a graceful deer—may her breasts satisfy you always, may you ever be intoxicated with her love" (Prov. 5:18–19). Solomon is saying, "May you be turned on by your wife." Sexual attraction to one's husband or wife is God's will. It's God's desire. In many Bibles, that entire chapter of Proverbs is titled as a warning against adultery, but that is the wrong emphasis. It's an important theme of the passage, but the emphasis not often preached in churches should be on the beauty, desirability, and sexiness of one's own wife in contrast to the deception and destructiveness of sexual pursuits outside of marriage.

Let's turn to New Testament times to see how the apostle Paul discusses sexuality.

Sex and the early Church: In 1 Corinthians 7, Paul is addressing some questions and dysfunctions in the Church concerning their view of sex. We need to remember that we don't live in the most sex-saturated time in history, even though the internet might make it seem otherwise. Other times and places have seen sex elevated in unhealthy ways.

If you came to know Christ in Corinth, you lived in a XXX culture. There were temples on every corner where spirituality and sexuality were offered in a toxic mix. In most of their pagan religions, prostitutes—both male and female—were part of their religious rituals. The ancient world, all the way back to the Canaanites who occupied the Promised Land, featured temple prostitutes, distorted ideas of fertility, and child sacrifice. This pattern of sexual distortions and religion was prevalent throughout much of the Old Testament, and it was alive and causing damage in the first century too.

When Paul arrived in Corinth, people heard the gospel and trusted Christ. As they came to know Jesus as the Messiah and the forgiver of their sins and began to follow Him, they brought with them their sexually distorted background. Two major errors dominated the view of sex within the Church. One group of Corinthians came into Christianity with a view of physical matters expressed in the saying, "Food for the stomach and the stomach for food" (1 Cor. 6:13). In other words, if you have a sensual desire, like wanting food, God gave you that desire for food, so satisfy it. If you want sex, you should have sex anytime, anywhere, with anyone. That's how they grew up.

To this group Paul essentially writes, "No, that premise may seem logical, but it misses God's design and purpose for sex." The apostle explains that sex is sacred and God places it in a very special and unique environment for our joy and protection. Sex functions like the fire in a fireplace. God wants the fire to burn hot and passionate inside the fireplace of marriage, where it brings light, heat, warmth, and intimacy. But when the fire is taken out of the fireplace to places it shouldn't be, it destroys, and its purpose is also destroyed.

> **Sex functions like the fire in a fireplace. God wants the fire to burn hot and passionate inside the fireplace of marriage, where it brings light, heat, warmth, and intimacy.**

The other worldview that influenced the Corinthians wasn't sex anytime with anyone. It was distorted in the opposite direction. The Greek philosophy of dualism had taken hold with many Corinthians. Dualism teaches that the body and the material world are evil and the spirit and the immaterial world are good. When these new believers came to Christ, they reasoned, "We're not going to have sex, even inside of our marriage, because it's impure and unholy. Sex has to do with the body, so it's evil."

To the dualists, the apostle Paul wrote:

> But since sexual immorality is occurring, each man should have sexual relations with his own wife, and each woman with her own husband. The husband should fulfill his marital duty to his wife, and likewise the wife to her husband. The wife does not have authority over her own body but yields it to her husband. In the same way, the husband does not have authority over his own body but yields it to his wife. Do not deprive each other except perhaps by mutual consent and for a time, so that you may devote yourselves to prayer. Then come together again so that Satan will not tempt you because of your lack of self-control. (1 Cor. 7:2–5)

Paul basically was telling the Corinthians what we have not taught well or clearly in the Church. Namely, a husband and wife are one before God. You, husband, including your body, are to serve your mate, and she, including her body, is to serve you. Sex is a vital part of the marriage relationship, and you are not to deny one another except for specific seasons of prayer. And in these cases it's strongly implied that you should get together soon thereafter!

This radical teaching on sex was like throwing a grenade into the culture in Corinth. This view forcefully contradicted both the "sex as casual and meaningless hook-ups" and the "sex is evil" ideas that were influencing the new Christians. God was presenting a dynamic part of the marriage relationship that affects all of life. Far from being some small area, sexual intercourse is a crucial aspect of the bonding process. It's a part of the mental, physical, and relational unity that God desires in marriage.

Sex and Science: Dr. Walt Larimore, one of America's best-known family physicians, explains what happens in a man's brain when he has sex.[3] Researchers have discovered the release of a hormone or enzyme that promotes bonding in a man when he has sex with a woman. It has also been shown to cause a man to have a desire to open up, set aside his insecurities, and become self-revealing.

God designed the sex act in marriage to build an incredible core and bond in relationship.

God designed the sex act in marriage to build an incredible core and bond in relationship. That physiological reinforcement by design is one reason regular, quality sexual expression is vital to a healthy marriage.

I always get a kick out of the excitement over new, groundbreaking studies that actually reveal, "Oh, by the way, God's wisdom and design really was best all along."

Such was the case in an exhaustive study on sexual practices in our society in 1994 by the University of Chicago. It was the most comprehensive study on sexual behavior since the famous and influential Kinsey Report (whose results were later discovered to be flawed due to the prison population upon which it was based). The Chicago study became a landmark book, *Sex in America: A Definitive Survey* by Robert T. Michael, John H. Gagnon, Edward O. Laumann, and Gina Kolata. In summary, their research demonstrates that "everything people think about how sex works in America is far from the truth. The impression given by the media in TV, movies, and commercials would lead one to think the hottest, most frequent, uncomplicated, consequence-free sex is experienced by single people in the swinging lifestyle. Wrong. What we see and hear on almost a daily basis is a complete fabrication, cut off from reality."[4]

The report found that single people have less sex than married people. In fact, the research indicated that the people who are most satisfied sexually, have sex most often, and have the greatest satisfaction in their sexual relationship are those in monogamous, marital relationships. "The researchers even went so far as to suggest a link between traditional values and sexual fulfillment. They say their figures imply that an 'orthodox view of romance, courtship, and sexuality' may well be the one way to sexual satisfaction. They stop short of advocating Judeo-Christian morality but the data speaks for itself."[5] Apparently, Christians may be a little embarrassed to talk about it with their kids, but they're having a lot of fun in the bedroom.

Here's the truth behind the lies that bombard us from the world. Those whose relationships honor God's design receive the benefits God built into that design. Christian men find themselves driven to communicate if they love their wives. There's more vulnerability and trust found in a committed relationship under God's covenant design. It's not just about two people; Christ is the center of a Christian marriage. It's also true that contrary to popular opinion, sex is far more than technique. Satisfying sex is built and thrives in a safe and loving environment of vulnerability, trust, and serving one's partner rather than focusing primarily on what one can "get." The principle of "give and it will be given unto you" really works! As a husband cares and loves his wife she feels nurtured and, as one author says, she opens up like a flower.

The popular disdain for monogamy and Christian principles in marriage has led to less sex and less satisfying sex by those who disregard the wisdom of God's design.

▇ MYTH 3: As long as people love each other, sex is okay with God.

▇ TRUTH: The Bible prohibits all sexual relationships outside marriage.

Key Texts:

- "You shall not commit adultery." (Exod. 20:14)

- "Abstain from . . . sexual immorality." (Acts 15:29)

- "Flee from sexual immorality." (1 Cor. 6:18)

- "We should not commit sexual immorality." (1 Cor. 10:8)

- "But among you there must not be even a hint of sexual immorality." (Eph. 5:3)

- "It is God's will that you . . . should avoid sexual immorality." (1 Thess. 4:3)

The third myth that has saturated our society is the claim that as long as people love each other, sex is okay with God. During the years that I did college ministry, I had college students say, "I don't think it really says anywhere in the Bible that sex outside of marriage is wrong."

You've probably heard this line of reasoning: if two people really love each other, why does God care? After all, marriage is just a sheet of paper. Why can't we just be committed to one another?

The answer is simple: you're not committed unless you're married. You can say and even feel you're committed, but without the legal, public aspect of marriage, anybody can walk out anytime in that relationship. Private promises to be faithful that shy away from being witnessed by others and entering into the spiritual covenant and legal contract of marriage are suspect. Only 30 to 40 percent of those who live together eventually get married and maintain the relationship.[6]

The truth is that the Bible clearly prohibits all sexual relationships outside of marriage. Let's look again at the key texts for this section. Exodus 20:14 declares, **"You shall not commit adultery."** God forbids sexual contact with someone other than one's mate. Acts 15:29 states, **"Abstain from . . . sexual immorality."** **"Flee from sexual immorality,"** says 1 Corinthians 6:18. **"We should not commit sexual immorality,"** echoes 1 Corinthians 10:8. And Paul raised the bar for believers when he wrote, **"But among you there must not be even a hint of sexual immorality"** (Eph. 5:3). And 1 Thessalonians 4:3 adds, **"And it is God's will that you should be sanctified: that you should avoid sexual immorality."**

The root word for "immorality" is a very broad word in Greek—*porneia*. Can you think of words we get from that, such as *pornography*? In Greek the word was used to refer to all sorts of sexual distortion: adultery, fornication, homosexuality, and behaviors associated with those things. When it is used with a phrase like "a hint" it means fantasizing, lusting in your mind. *Porneia* includes such activities as petting heavily to bring arousal to a person of the opposite sex that can't be fulfilled righteously apart from marriage. It clearly declares that all of those practices are prohibited and morally wrong. *Porneia* refers to all sexual sin.

The great majority of unbelievers *and* believers are experiencing desperately second-rate sex. When He issued these commands about sexual purity, God already knew about AIDS and gonorrhea and herpes. He knew about emotional scars. He knows about shameful flashbacks when you're having sex with someone and you've had sex previously with four or forty other people. He knows about sexual insensitivity. He knows about all the pain that illicit sexual behavior brings with it. He knows that when you're sexually reckless before marriage the probability of an extramarital affair escalates dramatically.

Faced with the Bible's clear prohibitions about sexual immorality, people are often shocked. But the lesson is missed if we don't ask why God would be so adamant about steering us away from illicit sex. Do you ever wonder why? Since we know God is pro-sex, why all the restrictions? Why such strong prohibitions against meaningless, casual sex? The answer: God resists any notion that we can separate sexual desires or actions from the rest of life. God is jealous for our best and wants to protect sex and its sacred power for two people to bond in an environment where they know intimately and are known.

God declared the boundaries of the fireplace so He could also say, "I want to protect you. I want to provide for you. I want to give you the highest and the best." More than just an action, sex matters to God and He gave it to us as a sacred gift. He created us as sexual beings.

■ **MYTH 4: Only a cosmic killjoy, totally out of touch with to-day's culture and people's needs, would prohibit all sex outside of marriage.**

■ **TRUTH: God prohibits all immoral behavior outside of marriage because of His desire to . . .**

- Protect you (Rom. 6:23)

- Provide for you (Jer. 29:11)

Have you ever thought that only a cosmic killjoy, totally out of touch with today's culture and people's needs, would prohibit all sex outside of marriage? Now, before I answer, this might be a good place to tell you a little more about myself. I didn't personally come to Christ until I was eighteen. I had never read the Bible. I grew up in a moral home but not a scripturally based Christian home. The church I grew up in was far from Biblical or authentic, and I rejected church and God as well. Fortunately, He didn't reject me. I began my personal relationship with Christ after my senior year in high school and then attended a college where there were four girls for every guy. You could be ugly and get great dates.

My college years were in the mid-seventies, when "Make love, not war" was the mantra of the day. Everyone was sleeping with everyone. Life on campus was all about free love, and the sexual revolution was in full motion.

Meanwhile, God was working in my life. I was growing spiritually and reading my Bible faithfully. As I did, I kept coming across all these crazy commandments against what I saw going on around me every day. The temptations for me were real and plentiful. And

I found myself thinking, *There's this great fence and all the good stuff is on that side of the fence but God says, "No!"* I was frustrated and saw God as the biggest cosmic killjoy in the world.

I remember telling God, "You know, how would it be if I handled my relationship by school standards? Seventy out of a hundred is a *C*, eighty out of a hundred is a *B*, and ninety out of a hundred is an *A*. What if I kept eight out of ten commands? I could be an 80-percenter. I'd even be willing to be a 90-percenter, I think!" How could God ask me to completely pass on all the opportunities for female access that surrounded me?

God prohibits all immoral behavior outside of marriage because of His desire to protect us.

Here's the truth I had to learn: God prohibits all immoral behavior outside of marriage because of His desire to protect us. Romans 6:23 says, "For the wages of sin is death, but the gift of God is eternal life." What's a wage? A wage is some kind of payment in exchange for an activity. A wage can be a consequence. The wages of doing something wrong sexually is death. In Scripture, death isn't just physical death. Death is separation. When our first parents sinned, they didn't fall over physically dead; they were separated from God. Sin put a barrier between them and God. They experienced guilt and shame and began blaming and manipulating each other.

The light came on when the Spirit of God showed me the truth through His Word. Then, as I watched how sin or obedience was working out for other people, I realized that instead of putting a fence between me and fun, God was next to me with His arm around my shoulders saying, "Chip, that's not a fence with all the good stuff over there. The best stuff's here with Me. That's a guardrail. I just want to keep you inside the guardrail so you get first-rate sex. My plan is to give you the best. And the best part of My plan is that you get Me."

God essentially wants to tell each of us, "I want you to have sex without guilt, naked intimacy without shame. I don't want you to experience sex with flashbacks or scars. I want you to get the highest and best that I designed your body to experience. I want you to have the kind of sex in which you know I'm looking down on the marriage bed and I'm rejoicing with you." That's the heart God reveals in His Word. Here's a guardrail to protect you. But it's also to provide for you.

God knows your needs. He created you with your hormones. He knows the longings of your heart. He understands your loneliness. In Jeremiah 29:11, when the outlook seemed impossible for Israel, God spoke to them. They had worshiped idols and were far from God. The wages of their sins had created a pile of hopelessness. Then God sent Jeremiah to say words that would come out like this today: "Look, it may be difficult right now. You may be single and without dates. You might be hooked on pornography. You might be in the midst of an affair today and you feel like, 'I could never break it off.' But I'm not done with you."

You might have what seem to be impossible sexual issues at this moment. You may not see any way out. But God says, "Look, you come to Me. I know the plans I have for you, plans for good and not for evil, to give you a hope and a future" (see Jer. 29:11). God wants to give you the best—intimacy with Him and healthy, vibrant sex within the bonds of marriage. Sexual immorality, whether it's visual, mental, or physical, puts a barrier between you and God. It also puts a barrier between you and the you God intends you to be. And it puts a barrier between you and other people.

God says, "I want to give you a spiritual reward. I want to give you emotional peace. I want to protect you from sexually transmitted diseases. I want to reward your life with the very best. I want to give you sexual fulfillment." If you are a young person on the verge of facing the world with all its temptations, God wants to keep you safe from the start.

We have a heavenly Father who understands the media in our day and the silence of the Church. He realizes that when you meet other Christians and they're living together or friends confide that they log on to porn sites for "innocent" and private fun, they present you with pressure to conform. God knows how easy it is to start looking at other people and then adopt their practices.

As you face those pressures, I encourage you to look closely at the lives of friends (and even celebrities) who live sexually impure lives. Ask those friends the Dr. Phil question: "How's that working for you?"

Ask them some of the following questions as they fit the situation:

- "How did the affair work out in terms of your finances?"

- "How did the affair work out for your kids?"

- "What is it like to log on and feel like you can't wait to imagine sex with someone who isn't real?"

- "How does it feel to have your life consumed by secrets and shame you are desperately trying to hide?"

- "What does it feel like to read romance novels and have such dreams and fantasies about people who don't exist that you become so convinced you're sexually unfulfilled in your marriage?"

- "What does it feel like to have your thoughts continually controlled by sexual images that leave you guilty and hating yourself?"

Too often, even in Christian marriages, time reveals that many relationships began with a lot of hidden baggage that undermined honesty and transparency. What was exciting because it was illegal, illicit, and hidden suddenly becomes boring and shameful. I think our God would say in a gentle voice to all of the above, "How's that working for you? Don't you want better? Don't you want the best?"

We all have things in our past we are not proud of. God wants to cover those things in His forgiveness.

So often, when churches do talk about sex, the central message is, "Shame for past behavior! Here are the rules and warnings!" The application is, "Don't do this, don't do that, and don't hang around with those who do." That's not my intent here. We all have things in our past we are not proud of. God wants to cover those things in His forgiveness. He wants to help you start doing some really good things the really right way.

You may be reading this and realize it's time for a new beginning for your sexual identity before a good and loving Father, where it can be a clean, holy, wholesome, and fulfilling part of your life.

The journey begins with a first step. You will need to break some old ways of thinking and acting. I won't kid you; it won't be easy. You will need help from a pastor, a friend, or a mature mentor. Otherwise your intention to change won't last. Trusting God with your sexuality will take courage and faith. You will be swimming upstream, even in the Church. But you will soon experience the rich quality of life that Jesus, who died for you on the cross and was raised from the dead, promised to provide as He walks with you every day.

You're not, and never will be, loved by anyone more than Jesus. And He's not embarrassed by sex or shocked at where you've been or what you have done. He wants to forgive, cleanse, and strengthen. I encourage you to take some time to read about how Jesus responded to those who were sexually damaged in John 4 and John 8. You can be assured He understands and is willing to help you.

And don't be surprised if a few months or a few years from now God heals your life to help His Church be a model of passionate sexuality in the right place, in the right time, with the right person.

■ **MYTH 5: Everyone needs to sow their wild oats and experiment sexually before they settle down in a long-term relationship.**

■ **TRUTH: Sexual sins have a uniquely devastating impact on people's lives because . . .**

- It's sin against yourself. (1 Cor. 6:16–20)

- It's a sin whose roots are in spiritual rebellion and idolatry. (Eph. 5:3–7)

- When your sexual practice is opposed to what God says, you are worshiping yourself. (Eph. 5:5)

Let me share with you some representative quotes from many conversations I've had with people over the years:

- "So far, Chip, I get it. I understand that God wants the best for me. And I'm going to eventually do what He wants."

- "Everything you've said so far, believe me, I am really going to do that . . . in about three years. Ah, make it four. Because, I mean, you know, God's forgiving, right?"

- "I just can't bear the thought of missing out on all the fun and experimentation that everybody does."

- "I know He'll forgive me of whatever I do. So I'm going to go and have my fun, and when I get closer to slowing down and starting a family, I'll do it God's way."

Here's the truth. I say it with tears for those who have fallen for the temptation I just described. Sexual sins have a uniquely devastating impact on people's lives. Unlike any other sin, sexual sin can do almost irreparable damage to your life because it's a sin against yourself. When the apostle Paul wrote to the sexually confused church in Corinth, he had to say with astonishment,

"Do you not know that he who unites himself with a prostitute is one with her in body? For it is said, 'The two will become one flesh.' But whoever is united with the Lord is one with him in spirit" (1 Cor. 6:16–17). Do you see how sexuality and spirituality are always closely intertwined with one another? Our claims to a relationship with God mean we are subjecting Him to our illicit behavior. If He is in our lives, He is accompanying us during that shameful tryst, the affair, or when we lock the door and type in the address of the porn site.

Then Paul offers the answer and application:

> Flee from sexual immorality. All other sins a person commits are outside the body, but whoever sins sexually, sins against their own body. Do you not know that your bodies are temples of the Holy Spirit, who is in you, whom you have received from God? You are not your own; you were bought at a price. Therefore honor God with your bodies. (1 Cor. 6:18–20)

Our bodies and what we do with them is a very serious issue with God.

The holy, pure, awesome, all-knowing, powerful Creator of the universe, in the person of the Holy Spirit, dwells inside every child of God. When you decide to have illicit sex or demean the gift with pornography, it's like going into the most awe-inspiring church you've ever seen, filled with stained-glass windows, then using a hammer to destroy all that beauty. It's like driving a bright red Ferrari down the highway and deciding, "I'm going to go off-road with it like a Jeep." *Boom, boom, ba-boom, boom.* And just messing it up. That's what happens when you have sex outside the bonds of marriage. That's what happens when you fantasize. That's what happens when you look at porn. Your heavenly Father who is absolutely pure and holy wants to dwell with you, but you cut yourself off from Him.

There's a reason why your prayers don't get answered. There's a reason why when you open and read the Bible you don't sense or hear God speaking to you. Although God is ready to forgive and listen the moment we seek His heart, habitual sexual disobedience causes God to close His ears. It cuts off your ability to hear His voice and experience His presence (see Isa. 59:1–2).

God grieves over us and is jealous for His children. In His love He disciplines with the velvet vise of pain and consequences, hoping we will realize that what we are doing is unacceptable. What scares me the most today is that sexual immorality, in all of its forms—fornication, adultery, homosexuality, pornography, and lust—has become so acceptable in the Church today that we have lost our moral distinctive and as a result our platform to share the Good News. There's a reason why the Church is largely impotent today. We are spiritually ineffective in an increasingly violent and decadent culture, not because we're *like* the culture, but because we're *worse* than the culture. We know better!

Sexual immorality has become so acceptable in the Church today that we have lost our moral distinctive and as a result our platform to share the Good News.

Each of us is part of the beautiful bride of Christ. Your physical body is holy to God. He wants to dwell in it. He's not against sex.

Some of you are getting such second-rate, lame sex. He cries out today and says, "Stop it. It's devastating. It's a sin against your own body, psychologically, physically, and spiritually."

What are His warnings in Scripture and how should we respond?

God's loving warnings: Beyond the damage to self, sexual sin has its roots in spiritual rebellion and idolatry. There's a part of us that says, "No one's going to tell me what to do, God. I've got these impulses. I've got these drives."

This was me as a brand-new Christian during my freshman year in college. I started reading these verses and I reacted, "Hey, God, You know what? You can run the universe but You're not running this part of my life."

When you say to God, "I'm doing my thing my way," you have taken a flying leap into the middle of rebellion. In the Bible, when you rebel it's real serious. The apostle Paul, in Ephesians 5, makes the connection between rebellion, sexual sin, and idolatry. He was writing to Christians in another sex-saturated city. The temple of Diana was there, with a full complement of prostitutes and other debauchery. These people had come to Christ in a decadent, sexual world. **"But among you,"** he says, **"there must not be even a hint of sexual immorality, or of any kind of impurity, or of greed"** (Eph. 5:3). That last word refers to sexual greed, lustfulness. Paul goes on to offer his reason: **"because these are improper for God's holy people."** Then he shifts from their behavior to their speech.

> Nor should there be obscenity, foolish talk or coarse joking, which are out of place, but rather thanksgiving. For of this you can be sure [notice how serious this gets]: No immoral, impure or greedy

person—such a person is an idolater—has any inheritance in the kingdom of Christ and of God. Let no one deceive you with empty words, for because of such things God's wrath comes on those who are disobedient. Therefore do not be partners with them. (Eph. 5:4–7)

Now I want you to hear very carefully what I'm saying and what I'm *not* saying. When your sexual practice—in your mind, out of your lips, with your body—is opposed to what God says, He wants you to understand you are worshiping you rather than Him. Whether it's using people or viewing things, you are the center, and you are dominated by a distorted lust for something you cannot achieve on your own. I've heard it said, "Every man who walks into a brothel is taking a first step toward God."[7] Those pursuits offer a false intimacy that never satisfies. Longing for God is never settled unless we're longing for the real God. Any other pursuit is worshiping yourself. And it's actually spiritual rebellion. It's rejecting God. Because spirituality and sexuality are so closely linked.

Options for change: Going back to Paul's words to the Ephesians, where he says, **"No immoral, impure or greedy person"** (5:5), he's talking about habits and patterns. He doesn't mean you don't slip and occasionally reveal the possibility we all have of being that kind of person. But if Paul is describing the ongoing practices in your life, then he and the rest of Scripture say there are two options for you.

Number one is that you are a genuine, born-again believer of Jesus, but over time you've compromised repeatedly to the point where you are trapped in dysfunctional sexuality and you need to repent as fast as you can. You can't claim authentic belief in Christ while deliberately pursuing sin.

Number two is that you've been living with a misconception about your relationship with Christ. Maybe you've prayed a prayer, raised a hand, and reached an intellectual agreement with the gospel. You would say, "Oh, I believe in Jesus, intellectually. I believe He died, rose from the dead, and I prayed a prayer once. I actually go to church." Intellectual assent is part of faith, but not the whole thing. Trusting in Christ is life-changing, and it continues to be life-changing as we fall and He helps us get up and continue.

When the Holy Spirit comes inside of your mortal body, He creates a desire for holiness. And if, habitually, your sexual sin demonstrates no desire for holiness, or for God's Word, or to move the direction He has told you, then He says, **"Examine [yourself] to see whether you are in the faith"** (2 Cor. 13:5). Because Jesus said, **"A tree is recognized by its fruit"** (Matt. 12:33). If the fruit of your life is progressive, habitual, sexual immorality, then you need to really ask yourself, "Does the Holy Spirit live in me?"

■ MYTH 6: It's too late for me; sexual sin is so powerful, nothing can loosen its grip on my life.

■ TRUTH: Christ died to pay for the penalty of your sin and break its power in your life.

This final myth is one where I'm imagining some readers might be right now. You've read all this and you're feeling hopeless. You're not even sure you *want* to give up your sexual sin, though you now realize God is offering you truth you may not have ever considered. Please read on.

I remember playing basketball one summer thirty years ago with a guy from USC, a great athlete. One of those good-looking, surfer-type guys who has California written all over them. After a game one night I asked, "Tell me, how did you come to Christ?"

He started, "You know," then he stopped and gathered himself, and I realized I was about to hear a significant story. He stood there looking like some guy who should be on a poster, and yet his voice came out with a broken humility. He said, "There was a time a few years back when I didn't have sex every day—I had sex multiple times a day, with as many women as possible, in high school and throughout college. Women were available and I helped myself. I actually got so numb to what I was doing that I sometimes had sex and didn't feel anything. At that point I got deathly afraid because I realized the only thing that could give me the sexual buzz would be to begin exploring perversion, and that step scared me." He stopped for a moment, then continued, "I remember crying out to God and saying, 'I'm a prisoner, will someone please help me?' even though I didn't think there was any help. But shortly after that, through a friend, God brought Jesus to my life."

Christ died to pay for the penalty of your sin and break its power in your life.

You may think there's no hope for you. You say, "I'm too far gone. I've been in this mess for years. You have no idea where I've been and what I've done." What you are saying may be true, but it doesn't have to be the end of your story. Here's what I want you to understand: Christ died to pay for the penalty of your sin and break its power in your life. While you and I were yet sinners, Christ died for us. Before you committed any sins He loved you, and He still loves you now. And because He loves you, He doesn't want you to continue on your present course.

There is a heavenly Father who loves you, and no one is too far gone.

The standard is clear; the fire belongs in the fireplace. That's where it has to return. But there is a heavenly Father who loves you, and no one is too far gone. But to receive that love, and to be cleansed, and to be forgiven, and to begin to experience the kind of sexuality God wants, you must take certain steps.

Step 1: Be honest. Psalm 145:18 says, **"The LORD is near to all who call on him, to all who call on him in truth."** To be really up front with you, I had major struggles with lust in my early college years. I was stuck. I constantly struggled with where my eyes went and what went through my mind. I would cry out, "Oh, God, I'm sorry. I know what I did tonight was wrong." And the next day after more failure, "I'm sorry, I'm sorry." Then three days later, the cycle would continue.

I remember this seemed to go on and on. I was trapped. I remember praying and telling God how sorry I was and how much I really wanted to change. And I heard a strong whisper from the Holy Spirit. "Chip, shut up." Literally—"Shut up. You *like* what you're doing." I knew it was true. Things didn't change until I was serious about letting God change me.

I can still sense God confronting my spirit: "Get honest, Chip. If you really want to change, I'll give you the power. But stop playing games." That's when I stopped trying and playing and started trusting God to work in me. It made all the difference.

Where are you right now, really? This might be one of the most pivotal moments of your life. Is there a decision you need to make before you turn another page that will change the course of your life? Are you willing to be honest?

Step 2: Repent and confess. Repentance just means a change of mind. "This way I'm living and what I'm doing are not good anymore. I'm changing my mind." And to confess means you just agree with God about what He has pointed out in you that needs changing. The promise is that if we agree with God, if we confess our sin—in this case sexual sin of thought, word, or deed—He is faithful to forgive us our sin. But not just forgive, but to cleanse you, cleanse me, from all unrighteousness (see 1 John 1:9).

As a result of forgiveness, you will have a power in your prayer life. Being honest with yourself will give you confidence with people. It will be a journey. You'll have to renew your mind by a steady diet of God's Word. You'll probably need to get help from a wise counselor. Remember, what's the alternative? Living where you're living now?

Step 3: Forsake your sinful behavior. And then finally, after facing the truth, repenting, and confessing, you need to forsake that sinful behavior. **"Whoever conceals their sins does not prosper,"** Proverbs 28:13 says, **"but the one who confesses and renounces them finds mercy."** That means if you're having an affair, you don't just slide out of it. You tell the person today, "We're done." If it's a porn issue, you find someone of the same gender you can trust and say, "I need help. I'm going to address it." And you unplug your computer.

Whatever you need to do—be as radical as you need to be. That was what Jesus meant when He said, **"If your right eye causes you to stumble, gouge it out and throw it away. . . . If your right hand causes you to stumble, cut it off and throw it away"** (Matt. 5:29–30). He didn't mean it literally. You could pluck out one eye and still lust with the other. He meant sin has to be treated as a deadly danger. He was telling you to be as drastic as you need to be, to do whatever God calls you to do, because your heavenly Father has a desire and a plan to love you and give you what's best.

How about you? How have you thought about sex and your relationship with God? Have you bought some of these lies? Can you imagine sex as a sacred, intimate gift from your Creator to cement and satisfy your need for a love built on permanence, security, and commitment?

Do you realize that wherever you are and wherever you've been that Jesus extends an offer to receive His forgiveness and start afresh? You matter! Sex is sacred! Don't settle for less.

CHAPTER 4

HOMOSEXUALITY
WHAT DO YOU SAY TO A GAY FRIEND?

"Haven't you read," he replied, "that at the beginning the Creator 'made them male and female,' and said, 'For this reason a man will leave his father and mother and be united to his wife, and the two will become one flesh'? So they are no longer two, but one flesh. Therefore what God has joined together, let no one separate."

Matthew 19:4–6
Jesus of Nazareth

As we begin this chapter, maybe a little bit differently than you might think, I'd like to offer an apology to the homosexual community. As a follower of Jesus, I want to state as clearly as I can to any homosexual reading these words that I regret the treatment you have received from people who claim to be my brothers and sisters in Christ. I apologize that we Christians have, as a group, not treated you as Christ longs to treat you. We haven't loved you as Christ loves you.

I've been around this block for a while. I lived in Santa Cruz, California, for many years, and in other cities where large segments of the population were lesbian or gay. I've had to live alongside and learn to love not only homosexual people but also brothers and sisters in Christ who in the name of Christ have felt compelled to hold up demeaning signs, call people offensive names, scream judgment on others for whom Christ died, and declare with no hesitation, "You're on your way to hell."

The only experience of Christianity many in the homosexual community have had is with angry, bigoted people, some who have even been violent in their rejection. The absolute love of God has been completely missing from too many encounters. Efforts to compassionately express the truth about God's view of fallen human beings have instead done little more than convey hatred and fear. The stereotype of Christians as homophobic has not come out of thin air.

Believe me when I said above that I've had to live with and learn to love people representing both sides of this divisive issue. I know that as soon as I stand with or try to love people on either side of this conflict, I'm immediately seen as an "enemy" by the other. Even writing this chapter with the best of intentions has put me in the enemy crosshairs of certain people. Some Christians will think I'm far too soft and understanding of homosexuals while some in the gay community will think I'm attacking them regardless of how fair or lovingly I try to communicate. So if at some point in this chapter or elsewhere in this book you decide I'm your enemy, please know I'm commanded to love you. And this chapter is my heartfelt attempt to speak the truth in love.

And yet, so much of what "Christians" have said and done has been motivated by fear rather than love. I can understand why some people are afraid of Christians.

But that's only half the problem. Under the banner of Christianity, other groups say to the homosexual community, "What you are doing is not morally wrong." They claim the Bible does not prohibit same-sex relationships if they are grounded in love. "And besides," the argument goes, "the Bible is an outdated book not to be taken literally today. We now know better. You're not only welcome in our churches, but we will also sanctify your relationship by officiating at your same-sex wedding and conduct your ceremony in our building. We will even ordain you as our priests or pastors." In the name of love and tolerance, all sexual boundaries in Scripture are ignored.

These "we accept you" groups refuse to balance their emphasis on love with truth. They actually place a wedge between truth and love and withhold facts or Biblical passages that point to a serious problem. They seem to categorically reject the principle of cause and effect in life and go to extraordinary lengths to deny the reality of consequences in the lives of gay people. When a person's behavior reduces their life expectancy to forty to forty-five years,[1] is it really loving to affirm and endorse lifestyle behaviors with those results? As a society we don't hesitate to promote public service ads that say "Friends don't let friends drive drunk" or warn of the dangers of unhealthy eating, and when those don't work, to pass legal restrictions on people's behavior. Yet we seem to have a curiously blind eye to anything that's questionable or immoral having to do with sex. To not tell the truth about what a lifestyle does to a person is actually irresponsible and cruel.

> **Within self-defined Christian circles, we have one group that champions the truth without love and another group that champions love without truth.**

As a result, within self-defined Christian circles, we have one group that champions the truth without love and another group that champions love without truth. So how do we discover and communicate the truth *in* love? How do we put away the hatred and accusations along with the sentimental and wishful thinking that refuses to examine the facts?

A Supernatural Encounter

It was the spring of my junior year in college. A couple of buddies and I jammed into my little green Volkswagen and shouted, "Fort Lauderdale, here we come! Spring break road trip! It's going to be great."

We made the long drive from West Virginia, found some cheap lodging, and spent our days playing outdoor basketball under perfect blue skies, always with the sights and sounds of the ocean in the background.

The sun was setting one evening and I was already pretty tired. I went down to the beach and sat by myself on the sand, looking out over the waves. I had my Bible with me and intended to end that beautiful day reading God's Word and enjoying a scene He seemed to have painted in amazingly vivid colors. At that point I had been a Christian for about three years and was really beginning to grow in my understanding of God's place in my life and the direction He was leading me in.

Looking out at the Atlantic, I sat with the sunset behind me as the beach gradually emptied of people. But I noticed someone walking along the shore five or six hundred yards away, headed in my direction. That in itself wasn't unusual; what happened next was. Although at first I could barely see him, as I watched him approach I had an experience unlike any I had ever had before. This thought came into my mind: *Chip, that man is a homosexual. He's going to walk right up to you, and I want you to share My love with him.*

Like I said, this was a completely unfamiliar moment. I remember thinking, *Did I, like, maybe eat too many enchiladas earlier? Where did that thought come from?* Although it was very clear, it seemed random. I looked back toward the man again, and he was now about two hundred yards away. Now I could tell he was probably in his mid-to-late twenties.

Before I could decide what to do, the thought came again, almost like an unexpected whisper behind me. I would later begin to recognize that the Holy Spirit, at times, can certainly prompt this way. He said, *Chip, this man is hurting. He's a homosexual, and I want you to share My love with him.* Looking back, I think God was just trying to prepare me for a brand-new experience of His guidance in ordinary events in life.

Sure enough, the guy continued to approach, but when he reached me, instead of passing, he stopped, looked down, and saw me sitting there with my open Bible. He looked away, as if considering his next move, then walked right up to me.

Now, I need to tell you something. Because of my background and life experiences to that point, I have to admit that my first reaction was fear. I also felt awkward and kind of embarrassed. I remember kind of pulling my Bible to one side and leaning back on my fists, uncertain what to do. But inside I felt like something really bad was going to happen.

Yet even as he approached I could see this guy wasn't anything like all the gay stereotypes I had in my mind. If I hadn't been prompted by the Holy Spirit, I don't think I would have identified him as homosexual.

He began with a simple, obvious, curious question: "What are you doing?"

He seemed genuinely interested, so I answered, "I'm ending my day reading my Bible and talking to God."

"You can do that?" he asked, without a trace of mockery.

I invited him to sit down. He seemed to take that as an indication that I was ready to hear whatever he had on his mind. I listened as he told how he'd just broken up with his life partner. With deep emotion he confessed he was devastated and really didn't know where to turn. I remember thinking that it was so strange for him to choose me to open his heart to, and then realizing that the best explanation was that God had arranged it.

For the next hour and a half we talked about many things, but I began to share with him that there was a Person who would never let him down, who would accept him, love him, forgive him, and give him a new life—like He had given to me three years earlier. I was able to tell him about how God had used a very low point in my life to finally get my attention and draw me to Himself. One thing in the conversation naturally led to the next, as if Someone was guiding the agenda.

As the last glimmers of the sun were fading from the ocean waves, we bowed our heads together and he prayed to receive Christ. I never had to try to convince him he was a sinner; he knew it. He admitted his life wasn't making any sense, and he was ready to receive God's forgiveness and turn it over to God.

By the time we were done praying, darkness had fallen, but I think we could both see the streaks of tears on each other's cheeks. I was overwhelmed by having a front row seat for something God was doing in a person's life. I turned to him and said, "You know, there are two other guys here with me. They're also Christians and

they're pretty new to faith. I'd love for you to meet them."
We had planned this trip, not only for the fun, but as an exploration of faith.

He said, "Great! I'd love to."

We quickly realized we both had cars parked nearby. I said, "Well, why don't you follow me? The place we're staying is just a few blocks up the beach."

Once he got his car, I got in mine, and we started out. The streetlights had just turned on, but I could clearly see his headlights right behind me. After the first stop sign, I noticed he was gradually dropping behind me. So I slowed down.

The next light was red, but it took him awhile to catch up. When it turned green, I started out slowly, but he again lagged behind. And then I noticed his turn signal was on and he took a left behind me and disappeared.

Not surprising, a lot of people in the gay community are really afraid of Christians.

And I thought to myself, *Given what he's probably gotten from most of the Christians he's ever met, he's afraid.* Then I realized he may have been just as afraid as I had been on the beach when I was led to interact with him.

That was a long, long time ago. But some things, unfortunately, haven't changed much. Not surprising, a lot of people in the gay community are really afraid of Christians. And I have met many Bible-believing Christians who apparently really, really love God, but when it comes to homosexuality, and the homosexual community, they are terrified.

Join Me on a Journey

My goal is to speak the truth, based on facts, with and through an attitude of love. We must think clearly through this issue, examining the findings of both medical and social science. We must honestly examine what God has to say through the Bible and listen thoughtfully and openly to what the homosexual community believes. Our dialogue must begin with honesty and mutual respect. To take this step we must first understand the current situation more deeply, and second, work to become, as churches and individuals, a people committed to speaking the truth in love.

I want to walk through the two basic positions I described above. Please understand that we often approach issues with emotions that generate a lot of heat but very little light; no shortage of intensity, but a lack of clarity—what the Bible calls "zeal . . . not based on knowledge" (Rom. 10:2). To increase knowledge and sincerely understand the issues, we need to think through the basic presuppositions of both the homosexual community and those of orthodox, historic Christianity. Once we have a clear understanding of these two positions, we will be prepared to answer the question, "What do you say to a gay friend?"

Presuppositions of the Homosexual Community

What follows are the basic presuppositions that govern much of the homosexual community. Until we understand what people believe and what they presume to be true, we will never discover the common ground and compassion to deal with the issues rather than reject the person.

The first premise is foundational to all that follows: "I was born gay." This has become the accepted presupposition of most in the homosexual community. Out of this position flows a cascade of logical implications that build on the previous ones and justify the validity of the lifestyle. Here is the sequence:

(1) I was born gay.

(2) Therefore, homosexuality is my identity.

(3) It's who I am.

(4) And if it's who I am and I'm made this way, then everything about homosexuality is normal and natural.

(5) Since homosexuality is normal and natural, behavior associated with it must simply be an alternative lifestyle. You may have a different view of sexuality, but it's no more valid than my alternative way to live.

(6) And finally, if I'm made this way, if it's normal, if it's natural, then my sexual orientation is a civil rights issue, not a moral issue. Both genders and people of different races are protected by civil rights, so we, in the homosexual community, should be protected as well in regard to our sexual orientation.

You may disagree with the thought sequence above, but if the first presupposition is in fact true, then all that follows is logical and internally consistent. The choices and behavior it implies may be antithetical to your beliefs, but please take a moment to lean back and ask yourself this question: If you believed, with all your heart, that each of those presuppositions were true, can you see why you would feel angry or hurt over people who call you names, or say that everything about you is invalid, or even demand that you need to change?

We don't have to accept or imitate someone's behavior in order to "walk in their shoes" for a few minutes. But we need to remember that all human beings act in a way that makes sense to them. We accept or believe certain presuppositions that lead to our attitudes and behaviors. The fact that we disagree with the results of a thought process in another person's life doesn't excuse us from treating them with dignity and respect. As I have become friends with a number of people in the gay community, I've learned that listening and understanding where they are coming from goes a long way to building the kind of trust that allows us to dialogue openly and honestly.

Presuppositions of the Classic/Historic/Biblical Christian Community

In contrast to the position of the homosexual community, the historic Biblical position is that homosexuality is immoral, among the prohibited sexual lifestyles. The presuppositions for historic Biblical Christianity go as follows:

(1) Sex is a sacred expression within the confines of marriage between a man and a woman.

(2) All sexual expression outside these bounds is immoral and prohibited (these include fornication, homosexuality, adultery, and bestiality).

(3) By logical implication then, a gay person is not born that way, and the thinking and behavior is learned, developed, or

chosen. The Bible speaks in a number of places to the sinfulness of homosexual behavior but doesn't classify it as a category of special and deeper sin. It addresses lusting and/or acting on same-sex attraction in the same way it speaks concerning other sexual sins.

(4) The Bible doesn't teach that people are guilty for having been tempted with same-sex attraction any more or less than those tempted by heterosexual attraction. But the Bible does prohibit same-sex behavior.

(5) Biblically speaking, homosexuality is not something that you are (your identity); homosexuality is something that you do. What the Bible prohibits is homosexual or same-sex behavior.

Continuing the logical sequence,

(6) If homosexual behaviors are something you do as a learned or chosen behavior that's prohibited by God for your protection and for your good, then it's abnormal and unnatural.

(7) Far from being simply an acceptable "alternative" way of living, it's actually a destructive lifestyle. The Bible teaches and illustrates that homosexual behavior is deeply harmful relationally, physically, emotionally, and spiritually to its practitioners.

This leads to the conclusion that

(8) Homosexual behavior is a moral issue in which something "wrong" (like stealing or lying) is being promoted as something right.

As strongly as I know my friends in the gay community will disagree with the last sentence, this is the crux of the issue and frames any honest and sincere dialogue both inside and outside the Church. The place each of us starts must be clear. Here then is the question we need to talk about: Is homosexual behavior something morally right and good that is being unfairly attacked as wrong and sinful, or is homosexual behavior something morally wrong and sinful being wrongly promoted as right and good?

Examining the Premises in the Gay Community

With that question clearly in mind, let's examine the seven premises those in the gay community have been told are true. We will look together at facts from medical science research, from the Biblical data, and from testimonies from the gay community.

Premise 1: I was born this way.

In 1993, this statement gained prominent and popular attention when *Newsweek* magazine devoted an entire issue to homosexuality and scientific studies.[2] They reviewed the work of Simon LeVay, a professed homosexual, who set out to prove the biological basis of homosexuality by studying the autopsies of thirty-five people who had died of AIDS. Nineteen of these people were known to be gay, while sixteen were supposedly from a heterosexual lifestyle. LeVay found that the hypothalamus of the brain was smaller in homosexuals as compared to heterosexuals, and thus concluded that there was a genetic basis for homosexuality.

The acceptance of LeVay's theory was limited in the scientific community, as he was unable to verify whether those people in each group were truly homosexual or heterosexual. In addition, the variations in brain size were significant within each group, so his conclusions were not well founded. Many reputable researchers have found this study to be seriously flawed. Not only is there *not* a clearly identifiable "control" group in this study, but it assumes, rather than proves, a cause/effect relationship between the hypothalamus and homosexuality. It is just as possible to postulate that homosexual behavior could well affect the hypothalamus size. In summary, the limited size of the study and flawed procedure make the conclusions anecdotal at best, not scientific.[3]

A second study was conducted by Dr. Michael Bailey of Northwestern University and Dr. Richard C. Pillard of Boston University. They reported that in identical male twins, when one is homosexual, the other is three times more likely to be homosexual than a fraternal twin. Therefore, the study concluded, there must be a genetic link. The flaws of the study were that the sample size was quite small, that 48 percent of the identical twins were not homosexual, and that no account was given of shared early home life and upbringing or early environmental factors. Most researchers argue that the percentages work just as well against a genetic connection as in support of one.[4]

So the point is, if homosexuality is genetic, identical twins who have exactly the same genes should be uniform in their sexuality. They are not.

Here's what I can say about the genetics. Other research has been done, and in terms of all the literature available, although there has been a consistent desire to find links, there is no correlation between genetic makeup and homosexual behavior. Studies by Johns Hopkins University; Albert Einstein College of Medicine; Evelyn Hooker, a pro-homosexual scientist; and Masters and Johnson all deny there's any genetic link. They agree that the connection between genetics and homosexuality is a wishful myth.[5]

For example, it would be fair to say to homosexual friends that many of us have predisposition toward one direction or another in many areas of life that might not be best for us. The research seems to indicate there may be a predisposition in some people toward homosexuality even as others seem to be predisposed by type and environment to become overly dependent on alcohol. But the evidence of gay predisposition is far smaller than alcoholism. We know that almost 67 to 70 percent of alcoholics display at least a genetic predisposition toward becoming an alcoholic.

We all need help. And the same grace of God is available.

But we would never tell an alcoholic, "Predisposition is an excellent excuse. Go ahead and just get drunk all your life," right? There's a predisposition in some people for stealing or lying. But even if there's a genetic predisposition, another huge factor is accumulated effects of the fallen world we live in. All of us feel those effects in different ways. People need to be loved, understood, even when they may have temptations in areas that might not be our particular area of struggle. The basics of dealing with powerful temptations, whether they relate to lust, destructive thought patterns, or self-centeredness are the same. We all need help. And the same grace of God is available. But we need to get this on the table, and care deeply about people, so the truth and the love come in the same package.

Our guide and helper in this great task is Jesus Christ. He can teach us to see the way He saw. In Mark 2:1–12, four men brought their friend who was a paralytic to Jesus. His need was obvious. They went to great lengths to get him in front of Jesus, including ripping a hole in the roof to lower the man's stretcher. Yet despite the obvious need, Jesus immediately saw the real, deeper need this man had for forgiveness. He looked at the "stuck" man and said, "Your sins are forgiven" (v. 9). When we deal with people as they present themselves to us, we need to develop Jesus's capacity for looking past the obvious to meet the real need, so that the obvious need can be taken care of also.

Now, what you need to understand, though, is that in the popular culture the myth of complete genetic determination is seen as accepted fact. Realize that hearing anything repeated long enough and loud enough can make it begin to sound like the truth. The unchangeable fate of genetics is what has been championed by the gay community and repeated often by public education. But frequency of repetition or increasing familiarity doesn't equal truth. For centuries it was taken as unquestionable truth that the earth was flat. Many people can fervently believe what is not true.

And yet young people from a Bible-teaching church who go to school and talk to a friend are told, "Those feelings, that attraction you have for the same sex you just mentioned? You're a homosexual. And you were born that way. There's no choice but to act on those feelings."

When honestly questioning the most basic premise of the homosexual community, the following question is valid, whether asked by those inside or outside the lifestyle: If homosexuality is *not* due to genetics, then what causes people to have same-sex attraction? If we aren't born that way, why do some people end up feeling like they *are* that way?

When you review the research, you find there are several significant factors that influence a person who struggles with same-sex attraction.

The father's role. The relationship between sexual identity and the father's role is a huge factor in a child's life. Explore the background of active homosexuals and you will often discover a family background that involves an absent father, abusive father, disengaged father, or smothering mother.[6] There are often instances of early sexual abuse. Last night I talked to a young man who just recently left the gay lifestyle. His tragic story involved a long history of drug addiction along with homosexual behaviors and an underlying sense of despair. He just talked, and I listened to him unpack some of the baggage he is still wrestling with in his new relationship with Christ.

He said, "I never made the connection between my early childhood abuse and my drug addiction to homosexuality. I just thought God hated me. It seemed like a logical conclusion, because I couldn't understand what happened to me or why. What I'd been through seemed to limit my options to self-destructive choices."

Developmental factors. As you read the research on families, you find there are lots of developmental factors that can impact later behavior. Children pass through phases as they gradually develop self and gender awareness. You may well have noticed that, when kids are small, boys hate girls and girls hate boys. At a certain age, the opposite sex has cooties.

I can dimly remember how I hated girls—until puberty set in. And then I couldn't understand what happened, but those little girls I hated were replaced by exotic creatures I didn't know how to talk to. Something had changed inside that made me want to get their attention.

It's during those preteen, prepuberty years and sometimes during puberty when some of these developmental issues emerge. Kids experience certain unmet needs or fail to bond with parents in a healthy way. Some children are exposed to damaging experiences from people outside their families. Incidents like sexual abuse can keep a child from going through the normal developmental process through no choice of their own. They can be six, seven, eight years old and have an attraction to the same sex without any context or support to help them sort out those feelings.[7]

When, during those formative years, children are told, "You're born this way," it may take years to undo the damage. Or if they are in a good Bible-teaching church (or a not-so-good Bible teaching church) that just hammers people and equates a same-sex attraction with confirmed homosexuality, great harm is done, often under the guise of holy teaching. There are thousands of people in churches who grow up with these confusing feelings and same-sex attractions but discover there is no safe place to tell anyone and no apparent source to get help. At best, the advice they get is, "Oh, you'll get over it." Or, "Date a girl, or date guys!" Or, "Here, watch this movie."

This is an important issue that we will discuss later. Developmental issues definitely play a significant role.

Environmental factors. A third influence on people's understanding of sexuality apart from genetics can be called environmental factors. The media has gone to great lengths to normalize immoral behavior. The level of graphic content on prime time TV would have appalled people a couple of decades ago. The standards have shifted decidedly toward "anything goes." Programming seems to have moved from trying to find subject matter and story lines that will interest and entertain people to intentionally developing themes intended to reshape the public's perception of various behaviors.

For example, a TV show like *Modern Family* features three couples, one which is gay. Part of the impression given is that homosexuality is not only normal but a much larger percentage of the population than is true. Movies, books, and reality shows are intentionally filled with story lines and populated with characters who seek to normalize homosexuality. The persistent message is that what we see is simply an acceptable alternative lifestyle and the message blaring in the media is, "This is normal!"

As this message permeates the media, education, and the culture, the standards continue to fall until almost everything is tolerated or accepted. In a recent popular Marvel comic, one of the heroes, Northstar, is marrying his male lover. Now think about who reads comic books and how intentional this "re-education" of our culture is beginning with our children.

If people don't hear the truth or if Christians are uncomfortable with talking about these kinds of subjects with balance and compassion, we are leaving little boys and girls vulnerable and unprotected in dealing with myths and cultural bias concerning the core of who they are and their sexual identity.

Some environmental factors that promote the gay lifestyle are subtle and focused on children, while others are at the center of the pop culture. The LGBT (lesbian, gay, bisexual, transgender) movement that celebrates bisexual behavior has a growing list of celebrities, movies, books, and reality TV promoting more and more license to have whatever sexual experiences one can imagine with whomever (male or female). The sad and tragic dramas revealed by the lifestyles of celebrities have created an aura of acceptability to shocking behavior. Today's teens live in a world where sex with whomever and whenever is normative. This is not about orientation but about lust and self-gratification.

> **Today's teens live in a world where sex with whomever and whenever is normative. This is not about orientation but about lust and self-gratification.**

There is a frightening aspect of this situation that is particularly tragic. It's one thing to deal with the responses and confusion of those who have lived through difficult times and have gravitated to self-destructive ways of coping, whether it's alcohol, drugs, fornication, or same-sex practices. But it is disheartening and angering to hear the frequent stories of people who have taken advantage of the vulnerability of others.

I have a very close friend who lost his wife tragically. His daughter was in college at the time and struggled as she was coping with the loss of her mother. One of her athletic coaches at the college, an older woman, consoled her. But in the process, the genuine friendship and support given to the daughter became confused and destructive when this older woman also introduced her to the lesbian lifestyle.

It's important for Christians to understand that many people become involved in the gay lifestyle for a very broad and complex set of reasons. Some are rooted in family of origin issues, others because of seasons of confused sexual attraction, and others in times of crisis when legitimate and loving support from the same sex shifts to sexual expression. When Christians blast homosexuality as simply a "choice" that sinful, bad people make, they unwittingly and completely miss the real struggles and underlying issues of those who engage in the lifestyle. Without the protection of authentic family love and caring guidance from those who call themselves followers of Jesus, they are often defenseless victims.

Premise 2: 10 percent of the population are homosexuals.

This widely quoted statistic comes from the famous Kinsey Report published in 1948. That figure was frequently cited as a verified fact in the early '90s when there was so much media attention on normalizing homosexual behavior. The 10 percent figure invites the argument, how could such a large part of the population be wrong?

Throughout the public schools where my children attended in Santa Cruz, California, the Triangle Speakers (LGBTQ) came in and taught elementary, junior high, and high school students that

"10 percent of you are homosexuals" and then shared their "coming out" journeys while encouraging students to do the same. The message was that 1 in 10 of you is simply genetically made a homosexual.

This statistic is an unquestioned given in our educational system. But what is much less known is that the Kinsey Report is not only more than half a century old, it is a critically flawed study. The 10 percent conclusion has been proven false. The subjects for that study were volunteers out of a prison population. Not only did this sample not represent the population at large, it clearly included a significantly higher percentage of people with dysfunctional backgrounds.

By contrast, in 1990 the US Census Bureau found less than 1 percent of the population to be homosexual. In 1991, the University of Chicago conducted an extensive nationwide survey and found that about 1.7 percent of the population are homosexuals.[8]

In 1994, the American sex survey, the most exhaustive piece of work done to date in this country about people's sexual orientation, found that 2.7 percent of the population was homosexual men and 1.3 percent was homosexual women.[9]

The steady repetition of "You are born this way," and "10 percent of the population is gay," may rhyme, but it doesn't convey the truth. These "facts" simply don't line up with the best scientific research, even done by those in the homosexual community, or the best studies we have about what's happening in the population. We need to share compassionately with the people struggling with their sexual identity that they have been lied to by our popular culture.

Premise 3: The homosexual lifestyle is a normal, healthy alternative lifestyle.

This next premise is a logical conclusion from the previous two. The key words are *normal* and *healthy*. The premise states: If homosexuality is a result of genetics and 10 percent of the population is gay, then the expression of this lifestyle must be normal and healthy.

Speaking the truth in love means telling people—as caringly as possible—the truth about the consequences of their behavior.

The gay agenda builds on these false premises with sincere and touching personal stories: "I love this person very much and, just as you can love your heterosexual partner, I love my homosexual partner, and it all just boils down to a difference in how we express our love." Although I don't doubt the sincerity of my gay friends who argue by way of personal testimony and long for it to be "so," the facts tell a different story.

Promoting the homosexual lifestyle as normal and healthy simply flies in the face of the medical and empirical evidence. Speaking the truth in love means telling people—as caringly as possible—the truth about the consequences of their behavior. Here are some of the sobering facts:

- Seventy-eight percent of male homosexuals have or have had a sexually transmitted disease.[10]

- A survey of more than 2,300 homosexuals in New York and three other cities found 37 percent of the men and 14 percent of the women reported having a non-HIV sexually transmitted disease.[11]

- More than 50 percent of all homosexual men are carriers of the human papillomavirus (HPV), which produces anal warts and can often lead to anal cancer, according to Stephen Goldstone, assistant clinical professor of surgery at Mount Sinai Medical Center, speaking at a 1999 Gay Men's Health Summit in Boulder, Colorado.[12]

- Male homosexuals are about 1,000 times more likely to acquire HIV/AIDS than the general population.[13]

How do I say to someone I really care about, "Whatever you want to do is okay. It's fine that you may only live half as long as expected life spans. And I don't mind that, like a domino, what happens to you will affect other people." By the gay community's own reports, 24 percent of homosexual males reported having up to 100 partners in their lifetime.[14] The *Journal of Sex Research* studied the profiles of 2,583 older homosexuals and reported an even greater number of partners.[15]

Now, to be fair, are there monogamous, loving, caring homosexual relationships, as purported on TV and other media? Of course there are. But the idea that these monogamous relationships represent the norm just doesn't correspond to reality.

The statistics cited above are scary, but if we are to be caring Christ-followers who take the words of Jesus seriously, we are not going to turn away from the critical need to speak the truth but say it with love, not judgment. Those caught in the grip of same-sex behavior need to be understood. And they need to be loved.

Much of their behavior and struggle isn't any different than your behavior or mine in our areas of sinfulness.

Warning: The next few paragraphs are graphic in nature.

Before we continue, it would be a disservice not to discuss the sexual practices of homosexuals. I do not share this to be shocking or distasteful, but our understanding of the "gay" lifestyle has been shaped by media airbrushing to the point that we now have ethereal pictures that are not honest and clear about the sexual practices of homosexuals, and why they are so devastating to the human body.

The high rate of disease among homosexual males is due to unhealthy sexual practices. Ninety-eight percent of homosexuals engage in oral sex, and 90 percent practice anal sex with their partner. This is biological suicide since the rectum was not designed to accommodate a thrusting penis.

A report in 2001 from the US Center for Disease Control and Prevention revealed that 46 percent of homosexual men had participated in unprotected anal sex in the six months prior to the study. During such activities the anal wall is torn and bruised, giving sperm and germs direct access to the bloodstream. Since the anal wall is only one cell thick, sperm quickly penetrate the wall, causing massive immunological damage to the body's T and B cell defense mechanisms. This doesn't happen during vaginal sex because of the multilayered cell construction of the vagina.

When men have sex with men, or women have sex with women, the very actions are destructive. These behaviors violate God's design. The Bible is starkly descriptive when it says "Men committed shameful acts with other men, and received in themselves the due penalty for their error" (Rom. 1:27). Behaviors can't be separated from consequences. This is true for heterosexual as well as homosexual sexual sins.

Logically, homosexuality is a lifestyle without the ability to reproduce. Historically, there has never been, to date, a culture that has survived, a society that has thrived, when homosexuality became mainstream and culturally accepted. The anatomy of the human body, its design and reproductive purposes, leads us to understand that on intellectual, medical, and biological grounds, the homosexual lifestyle is neither normal nor healthy.

Ultimately, it's not a lifestyle; it's a death-style. But this harsh and unpopular truth needs to be communicated in the same way and with the same kind of compassion we would use with someone who was dying. Think of the massive amount of time, money, and research that is dedicated to people who are dying. We almost instinctively know we need to care about people who are dying of cancer, heart disease, and other maladies. Part of being genuinely human means practicing compassion with others and seeking to understand what they do and why they do it.

Premise 4: The Bible may condemn lustful, indiscriminate homosexuality but not loving, committed homosexual practice.

There is a growing and articulate population within the Christian community that has taken exception to orthodox, historic Christianity and revised the Bible's understanding of homosexuality to see it as morally acceptable in the context of a loving, monogamous relationship. Although a number of denominations sanction the performance of same-sex marriages and ordain practicing gays and lesbians to be ministers, this view of homosexuality is at odds with the first two thousand years of the Church's interpretation of Scripture. This has created immense confusion for new believers and sent a "Christian" message that seems to fully align with popular culture.

Historically, this has become the position of a number of mainline churches, and the view is gradually finding wider acceptance in more evangelical circles.

But what does the Bible say?

Although I will provide a clear synopsis of the Biblical teaching on this subject, I've also included a bibliography that reflects the way both sides of this issue approach Scripture. I find more and more uninformed Christians confused on this issue and overly dependent on what "experts" are telling them rather than engaging in the work and study of reading for themselves the testimony of Scripture. In responding to this premise, I want to summarize what the Bible actually says, directing you to the passages where you can verify these statements for yourself.

> **More and more uninformed Christians are confused on this issue and overly dependent on what "experts" are telling them rather than engaging in the work and study of reading for themselves the testimony of Scripture.**

The creation accounts in Genesis 1 and 2 reveal the intent of God in not only saying, "Let us make mankind in our image" (1:26), but also specifying, "male and female he created them" (1:27). The implied, clear design is heterosexual. The first chapter of Genesis offers a design summary. The second chapter describes a relational summary of creation. When God wants to solve the aloneness problem of mankind, those deep needs that everyone has to be connected, loved, affirmed, and understood, Genesis 2:18–25 describes the creation of Eve as the corresponding match for Adam, a heterosexual relationship. There are certain things that only a woman can bring out of a man and there are certain things that only a man can bring to a woman. They uniquely complement and help one another. And that's by God's design.

What follows is a look at five Biblical texts that clearly teach that homosexual practice, according to God's wisdom, love, compassion, and divine law, is absolutely prohibited.

In Genesis 18–19, we have the first record of the effects of practiced homosexuality being endorsed in a culture. The judgment of Sodom and Gomorrah culminates from escalating evil (Ezek. 16:49) and sexual perversion that eventually disdains any normal sexual practice. When Lot offers his virgin daughters to the men who are trying to beat down his door to rape his visitors, they reject his offer (as horrific as it was itself). Those who try to spin the Biblical account to soften God's view of homosexual practice explain this account as a matter of hospitality rather than uncontrolled homosexual practices. But the text makes it clear that hospitality didn't stand a chance against the homosexual demands of the men in Sodom. Also, as you study the passage in the context of the entire Bible you discover that Jesus referred to this incident as a historic case of God's extreme judgment (see Matt. 11:23–24). The issue there is wickedness as evidenced in one way by sodomy or homosexual practice. As Jude declares, "In a similar way, Sodom and Gomorrah and the surrounding towns gave themselves up to sexual immorality and perversion. They serve as an example of those who suffer the punishment of eternal fire" (Jude 7).

A little later in the Old Testament we find the record of God giving what we call the Levitical law. But the Levitical law is more than just ceremonies and details of worship among the people of Israel. Throughout the Old Testament, including Leviticus, the ceremonial law was given alongside dietary laws and instructions for the priests, as well as the moral laws God expected His people to obey.

God freed His people who were living in slavery in Egypt. Their deliverance included the dismantling and discrediting of Egypt's false gods, along with their vile practices. He guided them to a place called Canaan, where they were to displace peoples who were worshiping in ways that involved all kinds of sexual practice and included offering their children as sacrifices to idols. One of God's repeated warnings to His people was, "Because I don't want you to be like these nations and follow their practices, I'm going to remove them from your midst." Leviticus lists a number of very specific things that have to do with a violation of character and moral law.

Here is a key text:

> Do not give any of your children to be sacrificed to Molek, for you must not profane the name of your God. I am the LORD. Do not have sexual relations with a man as one does with a woman; that is detestable. Do not have sexual relations with an animal and defile

yourself with it. A woman must not present herself to an animal to have sexual relations with it; that is a perversion. Do not defile yourselves in any of these ways, because this is how the nations that I am going to drive out before you became defiled. Even the land was defiled; so I punished it for its sin, and the land vomited out its inhabitants. (Lev. 18:21–25)

Richard B. Hays offers the following note on these verses. "In this text the handling of the topic of homosexual behavior is unambiguously and unremittingly negative in judgment. The holiness code in Leviticus explicitly prohibits male homosexual intercourse."[16]

When I hear Christians refer to this passage, they often pull out only one verse concerning homosexuality. It's critical for you to get the context. I want you to see that homosexual practice is one of a number of prohibited sinful behaviors. The passage includes at least four specific sins, three of them sexual, that God absolutely prohibits. These sins will destroy a people and defile a land. God is adamant on this point because of what it does. It's detestable. Leviticus offers clear statements about moral behavior and holiness because His people are to reflect His character.

In Leviticus 20:10–21, another lengthy list of sexual and relational sins is included, this time mentioning adultery. God is saying to the people, "I don't want you living the way these other nations live. It is unholy. It's destructive." Many of these prohibitions came with the death penalty. By including the consequence of capital punishment, God gives us an indication of how unnatural He views the list of prohibited practices to be and how clearly He detests that which violates His original design.

Some will seek to argue that these prohibitions only apply to Israel and the Old Testament economy. They will often cite dietary or unique Jewish clothing commands that were particular to God's rule with Israel as proof that we no longer "hold to these Old Testament commands." Our rule then is to follow the consistent teaching of the New Testament and see where it affirms the moral law and commands the same.

So, moving from the Old Testament setting to the New Testament era doesn't change God's character. It sharpens the focus on the moral aspects of God's expectations. The level of sexual deviance that we know was part of the culture in the New Testament era rivals anything we find today. Our technical advancements may give us more access to sinful behavior like pornographic pursuits, but we should pause to realize the Greeks gave us the phrase *pornography*, which became the term for this area of sinful behavior.

Romans 1:26–27 gives us an unequivocal and clear passage on the verifiable consequences of sexual deviance from God's norms. Paul wrote these words while living in Corinth, where the brothel often shared space with a temple. On every corner there were idols, religious practices included the participation of both male and female prostitutes, and you could probably attend an orgy every night of the week. There were no rules. No boundaries. Sexual sin in general, and homosexuality in particular, is evidence of rebellion against God's design of all life and rejection of the truth in creation. So Paul was writing with those conditions in mind.

> Because of this, God gave them over to shameful lusts. Even their women exchanged natural relations for unnatural ones. In the same way the men also abandoned natural relations with women and

were inflamed with lust for one another. Men committed shameful acts with other men, and received in themselves the due penalty for their error.

Reading an indictment like this brings us to a point where we think, "These are strong, sobering words." Paul is making the case that a loss of wonder for God and rejection of Him and His creative design has resulted in God giving us up to our own ways with devastating consequences.

In the last passage we want to examine, the apostle Paul is going to talk to a church he loves very much. And he's going to address those who have certain habitual practices that they are unwilling to repent from, giving evidence that they will not enter the kingdom of God.

He is not speaking about people who "fall off the wagon" and have occasional moral failures. This isn't about people who want to do what's right. This passage is referring to people who by their habitual sinful practices say to God, "I don't want any part of You."

As you read these verses, I want you to notice that homosexuality is only one of the issues. Too often when I've heard Christians teach on this, I hear them read this text very carefully and then raise the volume when they get to the word *homosexual* as if the apostle wrote it in bold. In reality Paul is listing a broad array of habitually sinful practices that give evidence that the Holy Spirit does not reside in these people's lives. As you read the list below, think about the sins that *you* used to be most guilty of. He writes to a church giving them hope but raising before them a bar of righteousness.

> Do you not know that wrongdoers will not inherit the kingdom of God?
> Do not be deceived: Neither the sexually immoral nor idolaters nor
> adulterers nor men who have sex with men **[homosexual offend-**
> **ers]** nor thieves nor the greedy nor drunkards nor slanderers nor
> swindlers will inherit the kingdom of God. (1 Cor. 6:9–10)

What the apostle Paul does, the Bible does. There is a bar of righteousness for our good, and for our welfare, to provide for us and protect us. But that bar of righteousness is covered in the velvet kindness of His love and compassion.

Paul is saying, "Look. The bar doesn't change. Sin is an equal-opportunity condemner. We are all equally in need of a Savior!"

Considering this passage, I wonder what would happen if instead of highlighting homosexuality as being "the most terrible sin someone could ever get involved in," we just made fornicators the worst sinners. Or people who have been divorced. Or how about some of us idolaters? If you worship work, or worship money, or worship your kids, God says that's idolatry. What about gluttons or adulterers? What about people who log on to porn sites?

The apostle Paul is saying of all those things, "Guess what! Those are all in the same category. Those things will harm you, bring death to you. They will crush your soul, alienate you from God, alienate you from yourself, bring death into your relationships and into your body."

As followers of Jesus, we cannot ignore the overwhelming evidence that God condemns the practice of homosexuality. But it is just as important for us to recognize that God equally condemns many other sins, including immoral heterosexual practices. God no more condemns the gay person than He does those who have sex outside of marriage, live together before marriage, lust with their eyes, are greedy in their consumption, or swindle in their business.

As believers, we must treat homosexuality as we do other temptations and sins. We need to be forthright and truthful as we present the truth of the Scriptures, but do so with humility and compassion, not a sense of condemnation or superiority. Out of fear or taboo we often hide and fail to share the truth of the gospel with members of the gay community. Most of those in the gay community have never met a kind, nonjudgmental Christian who had the courage to share God's love and plan of forgiveness and eternal life. Just because a person is currently living in a homosexual lifestyle, it doesn't mean that he or she is not open to the love and forgiveness of Christ. Our message is one of hope, deliverance, and love. God is not trying to take away someone's fun or remove valid alternatives. God so loves us *all* that He wants to protect us and provide the best for us. If you genuinely love your homosexual friend, you will risk the relationship in order to share the promise of forgiveness you have received for your own sin.

> **Most of those in the gay community have never met a kind, nonjudgmental Christian who had the courage to share God's love and plan of forgiveness and eternal life.**

Premise 5: Feelings and attractions to the same sex must mean I'm a homosexual.

Nothing could be further from the truth. A typical human being is capable of an amazingly wide assortment of feelings—on any given day. Feelings by definition are momentary responses to life. They say *how* you are, not *who* or *what* you are. Giving feelings veto power or naming power is a recipe for disaster!

A man came to me after a church service and asked if our church would welcome his son and daughter. He explained his daughter was a lesbian and his son had "come out" the previous week and told his father he was gay. When he mentioned his son was fourteen years old, I asked what kind of relationship he had been involved in, and the father quickly said, "He's never had sex of any kind with anyone." So in reality, this young man and possibly his sixteen-year-old sister both have had some same-sex attraction and assume they are homosexuals. When I asked about any difficult family history, he rolled his eyes and talked about an ugly divorce, his ex-wife's live-in boyfriends, and mounds of trauma for his teenagers.

Imagine what it is like today to reach prepuberty or early puberty and have confusing feelings about your own sexuality. Unaware that these feelings are normal, imagine arriving to your health class at school and being confronted by the erroneous statistic that 10 percent of the people in your class are homosexuals. You are told these tendencies are genetic and therefore cannot be changed. Further, you learn that if you are having some feelings of same-sex attraction, you are probably part of the 10 percent.

Obviously, this line of reasoning produces powerful effects in the lives of our adolescents. And it is false.

As I've already mentioned, numerous studies in developmental psychology in tracking how little boys and girls grow up note there are developmental periods when sexual identity is being formed. In this developmental period of sexual identity it is not uncommon to have an attachment to the same sex. That a young person has same-sex feelings, urges, or fantasies does not mean in any way, shape, or form that they are gay. In the normal years of growing up, we all need to learn to bond appropriately with members of both sexes.

Those who fail to bond, who are abused, or who lack significant role models, may search for satisfaction of those developmental needs in other areas. This search may surface as homosexual feelings or as promiscuous behavior in an attempt to bond and be loved by others. These are temptations we *have*, they are not who we *are*. If a young person at the age of fourteen has a temptation to steal, this does not mean he is a kleptomaniac. Nor does it mean he is destined to be a career criminal.

In the same sense, if a young person has a loving feeling toward someone of the same sex, it does not mean that he or she is gay. Feelings of friendship or closeness can be powerful and should not be equated with sexual attraction. To suggest this is to do a great disservice and promote a powerful myth.

As I've talked with those who grew up in the Church and joined the gay lifestyle in later years, I see a painfully predictable pattern. Young people having the feelings described above feel isolated and trapped when they are part of a church that seems to relish announcing condemnation and even hatred for anything homosexual.

We in the Church must create a place where boys and girls, not so old and not so young, can say, "I know different people are tempted and struggle with different things." Some young men are tempted with pornography. Others with same-sex attraction. Some young people in their twenties have struggled in lots of different areas and met someone who has been nice, kind, and nurturing. If that intervention comes through a spokesperson for the gay community, they have found a vulnerable candidate for recruitment. If that intervention comes through a Bible-believing and practicing Christian, there is a safe environment to process and deal with the temptations and stresses of same-sex attraction. If they don't get open, honest, nonjudgmental love at the church, where can they turn?

> **One of the most difficult steps for those in the gay lifestyle is to recognize that homosexuality is a behavior, not an identity.**

Premise 6: Once a homosexual, always a homosexual.

One of the most difficult steps for those in the gay lifestyle is to recognize that homosexuality is a behavior, not an identity. This premise has been used to thwart those in the lifestyle from "stepping out" of it. The insistent message of, "You can't change! It's who you are!" is the mantra of the gay community. Both extensive research and the testimony of many people who have come out of the homosexual lifestyle refute this premise. The greatest hope for change, though, is given to us in the Bible.

The passage from 1 Corinthians that we visited a few pages back deserves another close look. I love this passage for my own life, I love this passage for people who are struggling, and I love this passage for brothers and sisters in Christ who have come out of homosexuality. Let's walk through it again.

Do you not know that wrongdoers will not inherit the kingdom of God? Do not be deceived: Neither the sexually immoral nor idolaters nor adulterers nor men who have sex with men nor thieves nor the greedy nor drunkards nor slanderers nor swindlers will inherit the kingdom of God. (1 Cor. 6:9–10)

Paul, I got that one. The wrongdoers—represented by all those examples—will not inherit the kingdom of God. The gate looks shut. End of story. But Paul *isn't* done. I love the next line: "**And that is what some of you were**" (v. 11). Such were some of you. Yeah, Paul, I'm on the list once or twice. In the same verse, he goes on to explain what makes the difference: "But you were washed, you were sanctified, you were justified in the name of the Lord Jesus Christ and by the Spirit of our God." The solution to not inheriting the kingdom of God and all that comes with it is not about what we do, but *about what God is willing to do for us*. The Father, Son, and Holy Spirit are all involved in the task of washing, sanctifying, and justifying people who otherwise couldn't inherit the kingdom of God in their wildest dreams! That's true for me; true for you; and true for those living a homosexual lifestyle.

As the Corinthians came to Christ, they had as much baggage as any of us could imagine. These people were not just homosexuals, but adulterers, idol worshipers, thieves, and robbers. They were people just like us; they were sinners. But Paul dismisses their past completely. At the moment they placed their faith in Christ, they were changed and made righteous in their standing before God. The God of the Bible offers that hope! Homosexuality is not a new sin, a unique sin, an unforgivable sin, or a lifestyle that can't be changed.

Once a homosexual, always a homosexual simply isn't true any more than once a sex addict or once an alcoholic or once a workaholic means you always have to stay in that lifestyle. Homosexuality is a sin. It's a serious sin like all the other behaviors in the list. And such were some of us, right?

I've seen this happen countless times. A young man recently introduced himself to me before a service and made the point of showing me the sermon notes on "The Truth about Homosexuality" and then saying, "That used to be me."

I said, "Really?"

He pointed to the man next to him and said, "Yeah, I'm glad I'm here. This is my sponsor; I came out of a drug situation as well. That used to be me, but I've been washed and freed by the blood of Christ." Then he added some comments that are gold: "But I'm on a journey. You know, where it says, 'Take up your cross and follow Jesus'? I take up my cross and I follow Him, and my cross is the homosexual temptations and thoughts that still come to my mind. I'm not acting on them. But it doesn't mean I still don't struggle."

Personally, I'm in a different place, but with the same kind of struggles. I'm a workaholic. I've been there, done that. I finally came to realize something was broken deep inside of me, and work was my means for proving my worth. But by God's grace, I've overcome that. I know that under pressure I'm tempted to be a workaholic. I've seen addictions to alcohol and their impact in my family growing up. We all deal with our brokenness and dysfunctions in different ways. But we all struggle, don't we? If we're honest, we all have temptations that pound away at our souls. Temptation is universal.

Until we as Christ-followers are ready and willing to admit those struggles and realize that some struggle with same-sex attractions, we will never be the Church Christ died to help us become. Here's a little test: How would you respond if someone in your church said, "Hey, I just want you to know I've been washed like you, but I'm still struggling with same-sex attraction"? Would you be ready to respond with Christ's heart for that person?

> **If we're honest, we all have temptations that pound away at our souls.**

Research indicates that certain factors help bring deliverance for those struggling with homosexual feelings. Help comes through same-sex, nonsexual, deep, loving relationships that nurture and restore, where brokenness gets healed and loved. Yet sadly, the Church has historically been strong on truth and judgment and weak on loving and caring for those who admit to homosexual feelings.[17]

God is calling us, as a Church, to a new day. The Masters and Johnson study talks about a remarkable success rate among homosexuals leaving the lifestyle when they get helpful support: 79.1 percent have immediate success; 71 percent remain celibate from their homosexual lifestyle. The research and the Bible both say, "This is not a life sentence that cannot change." It might surprise you that my experience with the homosexual community and much of my research have come from people who have come out of the lifestyle. Nonetheless, their honest admission is that they continue to struggle with same-sex attraction. Some have married and have children, and yet tell me privately that the temptations never go away; others have discovered that a life of celibacy allows them to honor God despite their strong temptations.[18]

When I pastored in Santa Cruz (a very liberal community with a high percentage of gays and lesbians), people with experience in the homosexual lifestyle weren't hard to find. We had a church full of people who had little or no exposure to Jesus or the Bible. Their backgrounds and lifestyles were all over the map. Many were from drug, alcohol, new age, satanic worship, and homosexual communities. Typically, I heard former homosexuals say, "You know what? When you're in the lifestyle and you decide, 'I don't want to be this anymore,' you talk about non-tolerance? Others in the homosexual community come down with rejection just as quickly as anyone."

For many, that experience confirmed that the premises they were using to justify their behaviors were indeed false. And if they come to a church that is authentically welcoming and loving, without excusing the sin or enabling sinful behavior, people who once were slaves to sin find new freedom and purpose.

Think for a moment about the church you attend. Are you willing to love the people God will bring, no matter what their appearance or lifestyle? In fact, are you willing to love the people who are already in your church who struggle with, are presently in, or have come out of the homosexual lifestyle?

We who call ourselves followers of Christ will never be God's Church until we address this issue, first with our own sexual purity and second with a heart that says, "We're going to practice Christ's love without changing the bar of righteousness. Whatever

God's Word says is a sin, we're going to hold ourselves account-able before Him." Ask God to help you do your part to make your church a safe, loving place not just for repentant adulterers and fornicators and liars and swindlers—but also for people coming out of the homosexual lifestyle.

Let me give you a glimpse of what it's like on the front lines. The young man whom I mentioned a little earlier, shared with me a little of the process God used to turn his life around. He said,

> The turning point for me was when a man looked at me and said, "God doesn't hate you, He loves you. And don't you think, if this was something He would want for you, that somewhere in Genesis when He talked about how relationships work, this would be there? And it's not there. He hates the sin but He really loves you." And a light came on. And I quit fighting it. And I began to investigate what it means to follow Christ.

Wouldn't it be great if more young men like him would meet Christians who know how to love and forgive because they have a profound and humble sense of the value of the love and forgive-ness they themselves have received from Christ?

Premise 7: All Christians are "homophobic" and could never fully accept a person who struggles with gay feelings, fantasies, or practice.

I can tell you that we have a very poor track record here, but I trust it's going to change. The tragedy of today's dialogue be-tween the gay community and the Church is that this premise is too often true. I began this chapter with an apology. Armed with knowledge and understanding, we need to move toward more open communication. Both communities need to rid themselves of the stereotypes of the past. As followers of Christ, we need to understand that the average homosexual is not "out there" but "right here" in our hometown, and he or she needs our love and our help. Most homosexuals are not leading violent marches or demonstrating in the streets. The average homosexual man or woman is a professional person with an excellent education and an above-average income. But this same person has deep, hidden struggles that are a very real problem. Many homosexuals don't want to be in the lifestyle and struggle to get out. But they fear they can't, or if they do, that they will be stigmatized forever.

As a Church, we need to communicate to the homosexual community that we are not only willing to "step up to the plate" and speak the truth but that we are also committed to letting love, acceptance, and God's grace rule our words and actions. We need to tell them that just as many of us have left sinful patterns and habits behind, they can too. We must commit to stand with them, overcoming our own prejudice and fear. Together we will see God bring forgiveness and transformation to lives in desperate need of healing.

Back at the Beach in Fort Lauderdale

I have often wished that I could step back to that beach thirty some years ago with the knowledge and understanding I have today. I wish I could address the problems and the struggles of that lonely young man, based on the experiences God has brought into my life.

I would tell him, first, that he was not born gay, but that I can understand how he came to believe that. I would tell him it is simply not true that 10 percent of the population is homosexual, despite all the false information he has received from practically every sector of this culture.

I would also tell him that his lifestyle is not normal, nor is it healthy, and would tenderly and compassionately tell him it will cause him pain, suffering, and most likely premature death. I would share with him that God clearly prohibits his homosexual behavior, not because He doesn't love him, but because it violates His design and brings destruction. And the same God wants to protect him and provide for him because He loves him so much.

Most of all, I would want to offer that young man hope. The hope that there is a group of Christ-followers who will love and support and understand him. The hope that others have made it through the same struggles and have triumphed. The hope that, in Christ, he can change.

CHAPTER 5

ABORTION

A THOUGHTFUL ANALYSIS OF A VOLATILE ISSUE

Jesus said, "Let the little children come to me, and do not hinder them, for the kingdom of heaven belongs to such as these."

Matthew 19:14
Jesus of Nazareth

Friday, 4:57 p.m.

It's almost quitting time. Home is on the horizon, and dinner with the family is calling you. You are at your desk, sorting stacks and slipping a few items into your briefcase for light reading later, when there's a light tap on the door. It's Debbie. She's twenty-nine years old, an up-and-coming executive in your company. She's on the fast track, demonstrating huge potential. She sees your briefcase, hesitates, and then asks, "Can I get a moment? Sorry to keep you, but I need to ask you something."

You stop what you're doing, set the briefcase aside, and invite her to sit down. The moment she asked for ends up being forty-five minutes long. Through her tears Debbie begins to talk about the man in her life whom she thought was going to be the answer to her prayers. He suddenly left her after discovering she is three months pregnant with his child.

She mentions, in passing, her career goals and schedule. She confesses she's never felt so alone. The loss, confusion, anger, and shame seep through her words. She didn't expect to be in this place. She doesn't know what to do. She looks at you through her tear-filled eyes and says, "I know you're a good person. And you're my boss. What should I do?"

What would you tell Debbie—and why?

After Church

June is forty-one years old. You really like her. She's been a Christian for about eighteen months and is still refreshingly rough around the edges. She doesn't know much about social graces and casually brings up some subjects usually not talked about in mixed company. She's a little bit loud. She has four children from two former relationships and has come to faith from a difficult drug background.

But it's so exciting to see what's happened to her life! She's really changing and growing spiritually. She has a great job now and is able to support her kids by herself.

"You've been a Christian a lot longer than me. What should I do?"

In a somewhat inappropriate way you've come to expect from her, she approaches you in a crowded hallway and begins speaking as you count the dozen or so people who can't help but hear the conversation. She says, "Look, I need to ask you a question. You remember when my ex-husband came back and we tried to work it out, but then he left for good? While he was here . . . I found out just yesterday I'm pregnant. I have four kids, I sure can't handle five, and I can't miss a day of work. You've been a Christian a lot longer than me. What should I do?"

What would you say to June—and why?

Tuesday, 6:28 p.m.

You sit down to eat dinner with your family. Wow! The day is over; it's great to be home, and the food before you smells and looks delicious. As you and your family pray over the meal, your cell phone rings softly, but you look down and silence it because you're not going to take it right now. Within seconds a text pops up from Amy that says, "I really need to talk to you tonight."

Amy . . . she is a sixteen-year-old girl; you've known her since she was four years old. She's the daughter of great family friends you vacationed with earlier this year. You've watched her grow up and become this amazing student and beautiful young woman. She has a volleyball scholarship ahead of her, and she just said, "I need to talk to you." You can't help but think, "This can't be good."

She comes over after dinner, and you go into the study and close the door. After a little "catch up time," she begins to relive the moment she was so excited about three months ago when that guy who is so popular and so cool asked her to go to the prom. The dream of going out with a super good-looking athlete turned into the nightmare of her life, when she became a victim of date rape.

But Amy felt so overwhelmed and so ashamed she didn't know how to handle it. She just shut down. She told no one—not her mom, not her dad, not her sister or a girlfriend. But because you've been her small group leader in high school ministry at church, she considers you a safe confidant. She's terrified because she has now missed two periods and suspects she's pregnant. She's too scared to get a pregnancy test and has been blaming her regular early morning upset stomach on nerves. With tears flowing down her cheeks her cracked voice pleads, "What can I do? I mean, this will ruin my parents' reputation. My dad is a leader at the church. My mom teaches women's Bible studies . . ."

What would you tell Amy—and why?

These are not imagined, unplanned pregnancy scenarios—they are real stories that represent the daily crucible of doing life with Christ. And regardless of where you find yourself landing on the issue of abortion, it's one of the most divisive issues in America today.

Abortion is not just a topic out there for casual discussion. There are always lives at stake. It's not like this is simply a theological issue. The fact is that 65 percent of all women who have abortions self-identify as Christians.[1] I mean, abortions are a reality inside all kinds of churches. So what would you say to the person with an unplanned pregnancy who is considering an abortion? How do you treat someone who has had one? Not just what do you think, but what do you believe and why?

When this topic comes up, usually it's like missiles being fired between two groups who can't even begin to hear each other. The atmosphere and attitudes are characterized by heat, anger, threats, and often violence. In this chapter, we're going to take a different approach. Regardless of your background, history, or past perception, I'm going to ask you to lean back, take a deep breath, and let me shed some light, not heat, on this divisive issue.

To do that, let's begin with some research. As objectively as possible, we will examine both sides of the issue. We will then evaluate where they have been, where they are now, and look at the evidence that supports each position.

I can almost guarantee that in the next few years you will find yourself answering painful questions about abortion from someone you care about deeply. I also realize that some reading this may have already had an abortion, and now you are wondering, "Where is God in all this?"

Understanding the Pro-Abortion/Pro-Choice Positions

Abortion today rarely spends much time out of the headlines. The legal struggle continues to unfold. But it's difficult to understand where we are if we don't have a sense of the history of abortion. Abortion has been with us for a very long time.

If we travel back a decade and a half, the lines between the pro-abortion and the pro-life movement were plainly drawn. The information from each side developed at the time addresses the issue in a clear, understandable way.

Planned Parenthood spelled out three basic premises that motivated their work:[2]

Premise 1: It's not a baby, it's a fetus. The literature spoke almost exclusively about the fetus rather than a baby. It spoke very little about pregnancy and focuses largely on the woman's needs and emotions and the impact of an unwanted pregnancy on her career, her future, and her body.

Premise 2: Unwanted pregnancy puts women at risk. The literature stressed the anguish, pain, and difficulty that an unwanted pregnancy brings into a woman's life. It focused on the situations of rape, incest, and abnormal stress, and highlighted the dangers of pregnancy in older women. It justified "abortion on demand" because of those reasons.

Premise 3: The woman is more important than the fetus. Most importantly, there was a clear distinction between the *who* of the woman and the *what* of the fetus. It was made clear that the woman is a "who," or a person, and the fetus is a "what," or a mass of tissue. Based on this tenet, the logical conclusion is that a woman should be able to decide when, where, and how to deal with a mass of tissue inside her own body.

Now, if we are going to move from deadlock and violence to dialogue on this issue, we need to understand this pro-choice presupposition:

IF a fetus is a mass of tissue (not unlike an appendix or a wisdom tooth), and **IF** you believe this with all your heart . . .

THEN the removal of that mass of tissue, if it is inconvenient, makes perfect sense. A woman has the right to do with it as she wishes.

Any understanding of the pro-choice opinion must begin with an understanding of the presupposition.

Understanding the Anti-Abortion/Pro-Life Position

Pro-life literature from crisis pregnancy clinics and other pro-life organizations have two basic premises upon which their beliefs are based:[3]

Premise 1: Life begins at conception. The pro-life literature states that life begins at conception. The focus, then, is on the need, rights, and welfare of the fetus. The life, the fetus, is almost always called a baby or pre-born baby. The presumption is based on a singular logic, that from the time of conception, nothing else is added. The embryo simply begins a process of development—a process, in fact, that continues for a number of years outside the womb.

Premise 2: Unborn babies are fully human. The literature holds that at conception, this life is a human being—not a fully developed human being, but human nonetheless. There is, in fact, no difference between a five-, six-, or eight-month pre-born baby and a newborn infant except location. To kill either is to kill a human being.

All the debates, the speeches, the fighting, the emotions, the hatred, the gesturing, and the protesting come down to one simple question: Is the fetus fully human life, although not fully developed, or is the fetus a mere mass of tissue in the mother's body? To address this question, we need to understand this pro-life presupposition:

IF a fetus is a pre-born human being (not fully developed) . . .

THEN it must be protected from externally caused death, under the same ground rules that prohibit all taking of innocent life.

These were the battle lines years ago: the issue was focused primarily on whether a fetus was in fact a baby or not. I have a statement from Planned Parenthood that specifically states, "To call the fetus a human being is arrogant and absurd."[4]

That Was Then—What about Now?

Technology transformed the argument completely. The sonograms of the past were crude compared to today's technology. Images then were black and white and grainy, and you could barely make out the form of a baby moving in there.

But technology moved up to 4D ultrasound. The image is no longer something that vaguely looks like a baby. Today's ultrasound images reveal an amazing look at a child moving, kicking, and sucking its thumb. The details are startlingly clear very early in the pregnancy. Even in the San Francisco Bay Area (one of America's most liberal cities), over 85 percent of all women who see this image when they have an unplanned pregnancy decide to carry the baby to term.[5] This technology has transformed the abortion debate.

Confronted with photographic proof that the old premise (the fetus is a mass of tissue, not a baby) was invalid, the messaging and arguments from the pro-abortion/pro-choice side began to shift. Notice the dramatic shift in the following excerpt from current literature published by Planned Parenthood.

> We all have many important decisions to make in life. What to do about an unplanned pregnancy is an important and common decision faced by women. In fact, about half of all women in the

United States will have an unplanned pregnancy at some point in their lives. About four out of ten women with an unplanned pregnancy decide to have abortions. Overall, more than one out of three of all US women will have an abortion by the time they are forty-five years old.[6]

Today, when you read the extended literature from Planned Parenthood, they no longer use the term "fetus." They talk about a baby or a pre-born baby. The message is: "This is the new normal. It's unfortunate. We wish there weren't so many abortions, but for very specific reasons, we need to keep this a real option for women." The focus in the literature now makes the central issue in abortion simply a matter of timing, viability, and what method you use. They recognize and admit they are dealing with babies, and the rationale for abortions has shifted to emphasize the rights and well-being of the mother.

The Guttmacher Institute is a national and international authority on abortion research, originally founded as a wing of Planned Parenthood. Much of their work expresses the core apologetic of the message of Planned Parenthood. Their language states: "The reasons women give for having an abortion underscore their understanding of the responsibilities of parenthood and family life." In other words, the decision to have an abortion means being responsible and acting with full understanding of the impact. As an explanation for why they have exercised their "right" to abortion, three out of four women cite their concern for taking care of another person in the family. Three-fourths also state they can't afford another child, and three-fourths say the child would interfere with their work, their school, or their ability to care for a dependent. And over half claim abortion is necessary because they are unmarried and do not want to be a single parent or the pregnancy is causing conflict with their husband.[7]

Whether the above sounds reasonable or irrational to you, I want you to take a deep breath while I do my best to reframe the abortion debate for today. I'm going to walk through both sides of the debate, using each side's materials as the basis for our discussion. Then I will ask you to walk with me on a journey to examine medical evidence and the history of abortion (which may surprise you), and look at what God says from Scripture.

Since 1973 over fifty million babies, not fetuses, have been killed in the United States with abortion procedures.

Before we go on, let me remind you of the three stories I shared in the beginning of this chapter. Although the names were changed to protect the identities of those people, the questions and decisions were real. How we answer the genuine questions of people in crisis is a real issue, a core matter of life for all people, but especially the followers of Christ.

Since 1973 over fifty million babies, not fetuses, have been killed in the United States with abortion procedures.[8] Fifty million people—a significant percentage of our population. Both sides of the issue would now agree these are pre-born babies. The staggering number is not a cold statistic, but a life-and-death reason why this is important to talk about.

Not long ago I was preparing to speak on this subject. A man in the audience stopped me and said, "I just want to say something.

I've looked at the printed notes you provide, so I know what you're going to speak on tonight." I could tell he was struggling with his emotions. He continued, "If I get up and leave, I just want you to know it's not you."

I said, "What do you mean?"

He said, "My mother was fourteen years old when she was raped and got pregnant with me. Her entire family and friends wanted her to abort me. And this fourteen-year-old girl was like a crusader who refused to have me aborted. And every time this subject comes up . . ." He started to cry. He said, "It is so emotional for me."

His wife sitting next to him, grabbed his hand tightly and added, "Well, I'm sure glad she did, because I don't know where I'd be without him."

This incident reminded me that this discussion isn't about statistics, numbers, theories, or political views. This is about life. It can be really easy to answer hypothetically as you weigh the evidence and evaluate the issue of abortion. It becomes very different when it gets down to a real, face-to-face, life situation.

Summarizing the Pro-Choice vs. Pro-Life Position Today

The issue today is, Does the pre-born baby have an inalienable right to live, under any circumstances, or does the mother have the right to terminate her pregnancy to care for her family and her welfare, both present and future?

The pro-life position hasn't changed. If the pre-born baby is human, then it's inconceivable to take the life of that innocent person. It amounts to murder. And since the woman now knows it's a baby, the case for premeditated murder could be made.

The pro-abortion position *has* changed. No longer is the argument over whether the fetus is a mass of tissue. Now the argument is if a pre-born baby negatively impacts the mother's mental or physical health, or the welfare of her family or future, then safe, legal, abortive options must be kept available to that woman.

These are polar opposite views that people are deeply passionate about. So passionate, in fact, that some have been not only vocal but violent with one another.

A Thoughtful Look at the Evidence

To gain any real understanding of the current debate over abortion, we need to look first at the history of abortion. This is not a recent issue that sprang forth in the sixties along with bell-bottom pants and long hair. There are, in fact, three eras in history when abortion has been "on demand." Understanding why abortion was encouraged and what forces supported and opposed it in the past will shed a great deal of light on today's dialogue.

Was Aristotle Pro-Choice?

The first era of "abortion on demand" was during the Greco-Roman period. Both Plato and Aristotle, while they believed that a child had a life long before birth (boys sooner than girls), put the welfare of society and family above the rights of a child and were strong proponents of abortion. It is not clear who was given the choice, however. Abortion and infanticide went hand in hand,

and the father clearly could have a newborn child killed if he so chose—a situation that often occurred if the infant was a girl. Plato's *Republic* made abortion or infanticide obligatory if the mother was over forty.

It was only with the spread of early Christianity, with its emphasis on the sanctity of human life, that the practices of both abortion and infanticide began to diminish in the Greek and Roman worlds. Christians in Rome became well known for scouring the dump sites for exposed babies and raising them as their own. An examination of early Church writings, especially the *Didache*, reveals passionate pleadings for the value of children and the value of life on the part of early Christians. Because of the convictions of the early Church and the transformation of the culture, these practices were eliminated for the next fifteen hundred years.

Were Nineteenth-Century Feminists Pro-Life?

History can often turn our preconceptions upside down, and what occurred in the mid-to-late 1800s in the abortion debate is just such a story. The early 1800s found abortion illegal after "quickening," the time when a mother could feel the movement of her unborn child in the womb. But after 1840, as abortion became more acceptable for women and more lucrative for doctors, things began to change. The birthrate in the United States dropped from 7 to 3.5 children per family by the late 1800s, with abortion terminating one-fifth to one-third of all pregnancies. Abortion ads were numerous in both big and small newspapers.

But two newly emerging groups of people aligned themselves to stop abortion: The American Medical Association (AMA) and the early feminist movement. The AMA had seen many of the results of these abortions and, because of the crude medical technology of the day, recognized a growing number of casualties from the procedures. Doctors were economically impacted, as well. Abortions reduced, by at least half, the number of births they could have performed!

But the real story is with the early feminists. Why were they against abortion? Early feminists recognized late nineteenth-century America as a male-dominated culture, exploiting women through abortion. When men were promiscuous, they wanted to "cover their tracks." Men pushed for abortions, and with no way to support themselves or their infants, women by and large complied. Men thought of abortion as a means of birth control and as an escape from any responsibility.

> Without known exception, the early American feminists condemned abortion in the strongest possible terms. In Susan B. Anthony's newsletter, *The Revolution*, abortion was described as "child murder," "infanticide" and "foeticide." Elizabeth Cady Stanton, who in 1848 organized the first women's rights convention in Seneca Falls, New York, classified abortion as a form of infanticide and said, "When you consider that women have been treated as property, it is degrading to women that we should treat our children as property to be disposed of as we see fit."[9]

The early feminists decreed abortion as a violation of women's rights. The AMA and the women at the forefront of the feminist movement teamed up to enact laws that outlawed abortion in America.

How Did We Get Here from There?

Today we are in the third era of "abortion on demand." After following the activities of the late nineteenth century, we might as well look around and ask ourselves, "How in the world did we get here?"

The pro-life victory of the second era was short-lived. Newspapers stopped printing the gruesome details of abortion, began displaying abortion ads, and stopped referring to abortion as killing unborn children. Doctors, having become uncomfortable with the rigidity of anti-abortion laws, wanted them reformed, reclaiming the right to decide what was best for their patients. American clergy remained characteristically silent on the issue, while promiscuity heightened with the advent of the "Roaring Twenties." Media and public sentiment shifted away from the rights of the unborn child to the health and welfare of women.

In 1959 the American Law Institute published a new "moral code," allowing "therapeutic abortion" in cases of rape, incest, and risk of mental or physical health of the mother. In 1967 the AMA and National Organization for Women voted and spoke in favor of abortion reform, and many states passed reform legislation that would broaden the definition of "therapeutic" abortions.

A curious media factor strengthened the pro-choice debate when experts predicted the world would starve to death in the near future unless population growth could be stopped. As a result, abortion became a strangely conservative issue, a crusade to "save the world" rather than a "tragic choice."

Soon the appeal for abortion reform became a campaign to overturn the law. In 1969 the National Association for the Repeal of

Abortion Laws (NARAL) was formed. Then, when public sentiment accepted the concept of "therapeutic abortion" but seemed
far from accepting "abortion on demand," the crusade shifted its
attention to the courts and the case of *Roe v. Wade* made moral,
cultural, and legislative history.[10]

In *Roe v. Wade* the Supreme Court overturned a Texas law that
prohibited abortions except when necessary to save a woman's
life. It determined that a "right to privacy" exists that protects a
woman's decision to have an abortion, and ruled that states could
not restrict abortion within the first three months of pregnancy.[11]

Additional laws removed virtually all barriers to abortion at
any time during pregnancy, and some sources tell us that abortion became the second most common surgical procedure after
circumcision.[12]

Approximately 1.2 million abortions are performed each year.[13] The
accumulation of each year's total since *Roe v. Wade* has reached
over 56 million in the US since 1973.[14] Under current law, some
states are *not* required to gain the consent or notice of husband,
parent, or guardian before an abortion is performed.

Medical Science

Where does that place us? Is our society one that permits the
wanton, deliberate death of over a million unborn children per
year or one that simply allows women to exercise free choice in
regard to their own bodies? To answer this question, we need to
proceed from our historical overview to the testimony of medical
science. We have seen that the moral discussion of abortion hinges

on the issue of *when* human life begins, and unlike the Greeks, Romans, and nineteenth-century Americans, we have the benefits of advanced technologies and modern medicine to aid us in our search for answers.

Consider the following facts:

- The heart begins to beat between the eighteenth and twenty-fourth day after conception.

- Brain waves have been recorded as early as forty-five days after conception.

- The mother can feel physical movements as early as forty-two days after conception.

- At eight weeks, the baby possesses the unique fingerprints it will have for life.

- All bodily functions are present at eight weeks and are functioning at eleven weeks.

- At eleven to twelve weeks, a baby can suck its thumb.[15]

Question: Would all of the above indications reflect a human baby or a mass of tissue?

The criteria for death as established by the Harvard Medical School may be used in reverse to demonstrate human life at early stages of pregnancy. Reversed, then, those criteria would indicate that the unborn is alive by the sixth week of pregnancy.

The criteria for a person being dead is (a) no response to external stimuli or pain (b) no spontaneous movements or respiratory efforts (c) no deep reflexes (d) no brain activity, indicated by a flat electroencephalogram (EEG).[16]

Using these observations of science, if the reverse of even one of the above criteria occurred, the fetus would be considered alive. At eight to eleven weeks, they *all* occur. The evidence for medical science is so strong that an unlikely group has surfaced to oppose abortions—atheists.

Take, for example, Elizabeth Cornwell, who is the executive director of the Richard Dawkins Foundation. As an avowed atheist, Dawkins and his followers have claimed to have a greater freedom in living than those bound by religious limitations. Curiously, they have taken an anti-abortion stand. Cornwell has been quoted saying, "There's a war on the womb. As a secular pro-lifer, I believe my case is scientifically and philosophically sound. Science concedes that human life begins at fertilization, and it follows that abortion is ageism and discrimination against a member of our own species."[17]

> **We now have atheists who are pro-life.**

So we now have atheists who are pro-life. In fact, when the late Christopher Hitchens was asked "Are you pro-life?" he did not hesitate to say, "Yes." He repeatedly defended using the term "unborn child" against those on the left who say an aborted fetus is nothing more than a growth or an appendix or a polyp. "Unborn child seems to me to be a real concept. It's not a growth," Hitchens said. "You can't say that the issue of rights didn't come into question."[18]

I admire these atheists for having logical integrity in this case. They are forcing all of us to ask how and why our species kills itself. How do you remove fifty million people from the US population and not expect to cause a ripple effect? The unspoken assumption is that all those human beings don't matter because they're silent. They can't speak for themselves. And yet I've met so many who, having realized how close they came to being aborted themselves, are deeply grateful to their mothers who had the courage to take a stand for life.

Modern-Day Idolatry?

When we pause long enough to realize that every abortion sets off some kind of chain reaction of loss, the effect is sobering. As the dominos fall one after another, it dawns on us that this issue is, in all likelihood, the most important moral issue, not just in our day but in all of history.

I remember reading the Old Testament as a young Christian and being struck by some of the obscure passages about the Canaanites and other "-ites" God was judging. The description of their pagan lifestyles involved the sacrifice of their children to an idol. That obscene idol most often was Molek, a false god they thought they could appease or manipulate by putting their babies in the fire. Even I, fresh from ignorance of the Bible and struggling to understand the finer points of the Christian life, read those passages and was sickened as I thought, *How can anybody be so twisted to willingly kill their own baby? How bizarre. How barbaric!*

But when we realize how we idolize our personal freedoms, careers, and independence today, it's not a far stretch to think of abortion as the modern sacrifice to an idol. We just have different gods. Our gods are the god of convenience; the god of, "Gotta finish school"; the god of, "Can't afford this"; and the god of, "I don't want my life messed up." This is a profound issue facing the Church as well as the rest of the world.

As I prepared this chapter, doing my best to look at this issue objectively, the statistic that most shocked me was learning that 65 percent of all women who have had abortions self-identify as Christians—35 percent Protestant, 28 percent Catholic. Tragically, 56 percent of all abortions are performed on women in their twenties and another 18 to 20 percent are performed on teenagers. So about 70 percent of all abortions are being performed on women age thirty and under.

The Biblical Record

Although the Bible has no direct quote with regard to the issue of abortion (i.e., "Thou shalt not abort"), the precepts and principles found in Scripture are crystal clear on exactly how God feels about human life, both outside and inside the womb.

Premise 1: God finds all life sacred and human life the most valuable and precious commodity in the world.

How can we determine the value God places on human life? Value is determined in three ways, and those three ways are emphasized in Scripture.

First, value is determined by creation and design. We assign value to things based on who created it. Try buying a Ralph Lauren Polo shirt for the same price as a T-shirt without a little insignia on the pocket. Or try purchasing a Van Gogh or Picasso painting. We place value on the object by virtue of *who* created it. Likewise, in Genesis 1:27, the Bible says, "God created mankind in his own image, in the image of God he created them; male and female he created them." God is the creator of human life. He took His stamp, His image, and implanted it on every human being on this planet. That gives each human being infinite value and worth.

Second, value is determined by protection. Clearly, we only protect things that are valuable. Dime-store trinkets, Timex watches, and costume jewelry, we may leave on the nightstand or dresser. Precious jewels, family heirlooms, irreplaceable treasures, we keep in a safe-deposit box. We protect the things we value the most.

Our world leaders provide another example. They are heavily guarded everywhere they go, from summit meetings to dinner parties. Security agents even surround them on family holidays. This is because those who hold the world's highest offices are considered to be of great value.

What kind of value does God place on His creation? Consider the protection He dictates for human life in Genesis 9:6: "Whoever sheds human blood, by humans shall their blood be shed; for in the image of God has God made mankind." God put the maximum social protection around a human life—the death penalty.

Finally, value is determined by cost. If you were offered a camera for free and could choose between a $5 disposable and a $5,000 Canon DSLR, which would you choose? Ordinarily, the more you pay for something, the greater its value. How much did God pay to redeem mankind?

First Corinthians 6:20 says, "You were bought at a price. Therefore honor God with your bodies." The price paid for you was the life of God's own Son—the ultimate price for any father to pay. Mark 10:45 tells us the whole purpose of Jesus's coming. "The Son of Man did not come to be served, but to serve, and to give his life as a ransom for many."

So God has said that human life is the most precious commodity on this planet because it was **created** by Him, it is **protected** by Him, and our redemption **cost** the death of His Son. The highest price that can be paid has been paid for human life.

If, as we've just seen, God finds human life the most precious commodity on earth, what if God affords the same priority to the fetus or unborn child?

Premise 2: Scripture affords the same sacred value to the unborn child as it does all other human life.

In Psalm 139:13–16, the psalmist declares,

> For you created my inmost being; you knit me together in my mother's womb. I praise you because I am fearfully and wonderfully made. . . . My frame was not hidden from you when I was made in the secret place, when I was woven together in the depths of the earth. Your eyes saw my unformed body; all the days ordained for me were written in your book before one of them came to be.

Even a casual reading of both the Old and New Testaments reveals that God was intimately *involved* in every human life—not only after they were born but before the earliest development stages in the womb.

Value by Design

How much **protection** did God afford unborn children? In Exodus 21:22–25, we find a detailed application of one of God's commandments as it relates to an unborn child. We are told that if two men are fighting and hit a pregnant woman, and she gives birth prematurely but there's no injury, then the men must be fined whatever the woman's husband demands. "But if there is serious injury [miscarriage], you are to take life for life, eye for eye, tooth for tooth, hand for hand, foot for foot, burn for burn, wound for wound, bruise for bruise" (vv. 23–25). God guards the life of the fetus with ultimate protection: threat of capital punishment.

Interestingly, this very passage is often used by pro-abortion advocates who claim that the phrase "gives birth prematurely" in this instance (v. 22) refers to a miscarriage and applies it to protecting only the mother's life here, not the unborn child's. However, a close examination of the text in the original language reveals that this is not the case at all.[19] Clearly the law protects both the unborn child and its mother.

What about the value by **cost** for the unborn baby? In Psalm 51:5, a penitent David reflects on his sin and cries out to God, "Surely I was sinful at birth, sinful from the time my mother conceived me." Here we see that sin is a matter of heredity existent in us prior to birth. Hence, the redemptive purchase price of the blood of Jesus

Christ applies to our sinful nature, whether we are a mature adult or a pre-born baby.

What are we to conclude from the Biblical record? That God views the fetus as a unique intricate work of His hands, for whom He provides the ultimate protection and has paid the ultimate price. Unborn children are the focus of His love, attention, and future plans. Their lives are of no less value than yours or mine.

The Bottom Line

My hope and prayer is that people on both sides of this issue have gained insight into the presuppositions of the other side. Until we honestly see this issue through the eyes of those who disagree with us, we will not stop "hurling stones" and start thinking through this divisive issue.

"Pro-lifers," do you understand why those who believe a fetus is "just a mass of tissue" resist interference with what they view as a "personal decision"?

"Pro-choicers," do you understand why those who believe that a fetus is a human life are so passionate about protecting that life?

Are you prepared to stop attacking people and start attacking the issue? Are you willing to "lay down arms" long enough to give a fair, logical, and non-emotional evaluation of the data? If so, let's suspend our biases and preconceptions long enough to examine the summary of the evidence.

Medical evidence shows us that although we can't pinpoint the definitive moment life begins, we know that the heart begins to beat at approximately eighteen days after conception, followed within eight weeks by the presence of all bodily functions. If we are intellectually consistent with our definition of what constitutes "living," medically speaking, the fetus is a human being, not a mass of tissue.

Biblical evidence shows us that God created humankind in His own image, paid the ultimate price (the death of His Son) in order to reconcile His creation to Himself, and places the maximum social protection around human life. With the same authority and assurance, the Bible teaches that God affords an unborn child the same rights and protection as a full-grown adult.

The medical community and feminist activists were at one time the strongest opponents of abortion.

Historical evidence shows that culture and trends have changed over the centuries. The medical community and feminist activists were at one time the strongest opponents of abortion. Could it be that culture and economics are what have driven these groups to "flip-flop" on the abortion issue? Is it possible that the data is clear but has somehow been lost in the rhetoric of other issues? Couldn't someone actually be a strong proponent of women's rights while holding the sacredness of human life in the womb?

Imagine with me a public forum or debate around the issue of abortion. After exploring all the information I just presented, I have asked representatives from both sides of the issue to convince the crowd to join their side of the debate.

Let's begin with the pro-abortion/pro-choice representative. The presentation begins with the four reasons they believe we must have legal abortion options:

First, because sometimes the woman's life is at stake if she carries the baby to full term. If we didn't have abortion, how could we save a woman's life?

Second, pregnancy as a result of rape or incest requires legalized abortion. How can we punish a person for being violated by someone else? They should never have to live with the horror and the memories a child resulting from that experience will cause them to have.

Third, if we abolish abortion, then all women will be forced, like in the past, to seek help from butchers performing illegal abortions, and many will be killed or maimed.

Fourth, it would invalidate the best technology we have. We live in a day when we do realize now, because of technology, that this is a baby. But there are times when it's just impossible for a woman to be a good mother because a child puts so much stress on her life and her family. We now have an abortion pill, and it can be taken early on, and it's very simple, it's not painful, and RU-486 is being used around the world. If you eliminate abortion, it wouldn't waste this technology for those who have to have abortions.

Now let's hear the responses from the pro-life representative:

First, C. Everett Koop was a surgeon general of the United States who practiced pediatrics for thirty years, and his testimony is that during his medical career, with the medical advances in understanding and technology, he was not aware of a single case in his own practice or his colleagues' practices where a choice had to be made between the life of the mother and the child. That argument is a "straw man." It's a very emotional argument based on a circumstance that just doesn't happen.

Second, of all the people who are raped, only .06 of one percent ever get pregnant. Yes, pregnancies do occur as a result of rape, but it doesn't take meeting too many people like Don (who shared his story about his fourteen-year-old mother being raped and refusing to have an abortion) to convince you that two wrongs don't make a right. A tragic means of conception, yes. But Don's life, wife, and family are all a testimony of the value of life even when conceived in the worst of circumstances.

Third, the thesis that back alley abortions are going to occur is false. Eighty-five percent of all abortions were done legally before *Roe v. Wade.* Only 15 percent were done illegally. In a given year, three hundred deaths of women due to illegal abortion were recorded. In the early days of abortion, 1.6 million abortions were performed a year, but now we're down to 1.2 million annually. Three hundred women dying a year as a result of illegal abortions would not even begin to tip the scales of the hundreds of women who have died as a result of legal abortions. Some of the recent court cases have exposed conditions in legal abortion clinics that make the back alley horror stories look like high-tech operating rooms.

Fourth, the RU-486 pill is far from easy and painless. It's not like a woman simply takes a pill and everything goes away. The process involves a series of visits to the clinic. And after all this, a woman will find herself alone in a bathroom aborting life from her womb. She will face one of the most traumatic experiences in her life alone, as she discharges her baby from her body and lives with that for the rest of her life.

In fact, what this pro-life advocate would say is, "What's never mentioned is the trauma and the pain that a woman experiences often years later called 'post abortive syndrome.'" I received a letter describing the impact. The young woman describes her journey:

> At the age of fifteen I became pregnant and my mother panicked, seeing only one solution. She took me to get an abortion. I spent the next twenty-five years keeping silent. I did not recognize that the subsequent cries for help in the form of suicidal thoughts as being a consequence of that sin. Turning to drugs and alcohol for refuge only postponed my pain. A double life ensued that no one seemed to notice: straight A performance by day, rebellious mind-numbing behavior by night. Eventually I married and sadly learned I could not bear children. Despite the inconclusive medical evidence, I could not help but blame the abortion.

In summary, it appears that there is no legal, responsible way around it: the unborn are living human beings, loved by God and deserving, though defenseless, of our respect and protection. When we move from the "frenzy" to the facts, that data is overwhelmingly and clearly conclusive.

What Do We Do Now?

Finding Forgiveness

"What if I've had an abortion?" Abortion is not the "unpardonable sin." Scripture is full of accounts of those who committed grave sins, even murder, and were not only forgiven by God but greatly used by Him. The stories of David, Moses, the apostle Paul, and others teach us that God can bring beauty and healing from the pain of wrong decisions. God's Word promises that if we honestly confess our sin, He will forgive us, release us, and walk with us through the process of healing. Without a doubt this is an extremely painful and emotionally charged issue, but there is *hope* for those who have been involved. If you or someone you love has had an abortion, or if you have encouraged or pressured someone you know to have one, please understand there is forgiveness and restoration available to you, from both God and from His Church.

As I have counseled women who have had one or more abortions and several men who have pushed their wife, girlfriend, or daughter to do the same, I am astounded at the depth of guilt, shame, and remorse that remains even many years later. I want to remind you that help is available, and the first step is talking with someone you can trust. The condemnation and power of the past over your life is "the secret" and the shame it brings. Get it out in the open. God promises in James 5:16 that as we confess our sins to one another, we will experience healing.

> **Abortion is not the "unpardonable sin." Scripture is full of accounts of those who committed grave sins, even murder, and were not only forgiven by God but greatly used by Him.**

Taking Responsibility

"What can I do to help?" With knowledge comes accountability. There are a variety of ways to respond to God's clear affirmation of the sanctity of human life. You may choose to volunteer at a crisis pregnancy medical clinic, become a trained pregnancy counselor, or open your home to unwed mothers as they carry their babies to term. You might write persuasive, articulate letters to Congress, help fund pro-life centers, help distribute information, pray earnestly, promote adoption planning, or remain informed. At the very least, we each should understand the key issues surrounding abortion and develop our own clear, factually based responses.

Establishing Limits

"How far should I go in the fight to protect human life?" As strongly as you and I may feel about our responsibility to protect the lives of the unborn, harming others or breaking the law are *never* righteous options. Bombing clinics, harassing and harming doctors, and taking part in violent civil disobedience are not Biblical answers to this issue. Our methods must match our message! Anger, hatred, screaming, violence, and graceless behavior harm rather than help the cause of Christ. The witness of every Christian suffers when someone claiming a Biblical mandate takes another rude stab at justice.

God's heart is generous toward humankind. He made us, He bought us with the life of Jesus Christ, and His desire is that each of us would know an authentic, dynamic relationship with Him. No matter where we stand on this issue, He loves us deeply, and He wants us to express the same unconditional love to each other. The unborn child, the teenage victim of date rape, the husband or boyfriend who encourages someone to abort her child, the doctor who holds the syringe or suction tube, and the angry protester on the clinic steps—they are all the focus of His specific, abundant, life-changing love.

I urge you to prayerfully consider the part you need to take in preserving the sanctity of human life in your world. Is there a step He wants you to take, an attitude He wants you to change, or a person He wants you to help? Please don't wait. Do you know the facts well enough to present them to someone else in a confident, winsome way? Please commit them to heart and memory. Or consider sharing this book with someone who needs clear information and a word of encouragement to make a wise choice for their life and future.

No matter where we stand on this issue, He loves us deeply, and He wants us to express the same unconditional love to each other.

Our world is in need of words and actions of love, grace, truth, and forgiveness. When it comes to abortion, they are an essential part of growing your faith, and for millions of unborn children, a matter of life and death.

CHAPTER 6
THE ENVIRONMENT
WHAT WE DON'T KNOW IS KILLING US

They brought the coin, and he asked them,
"Whose image is this? And whose inscription?"

"Caesar's," they replied.

Then Jesus said to them, "Give back to Caesar
what is Caesar's and to God what is God's."

And they were amazed at him.

Mark 12:16–17
Jesus of Nazareth

n my experience, few inquiries cause as much controversy and provoke as many polarizing opinions as when you ask, "What do you think of the environment? What are the issues? What's the central problem?" Bring up the subject of global warming, for example, and the sides quickly take up arms.

I've found that no matter which aspect of the environmental questions I look at, I meet passionate people who will give me amazing statistics and tell me exactly whom to blame for their concerns. But before long I uncover a different group or multiple groups of equally passionate people who will tell me the first group is wrong and then give me a whole different set of statistics to prove their point. Which media source I get my information from can radically alter my perceptions. The heat pours on, but the light dims.

For example, read through the following list of perspectives held by different groups related to the environment. After you read each one, ask yourself if that represents what you think.

- The central issue is to decide whether or not global warming is really happening.

- "Tree huggers" and environmental activists are basically liberal or new age folks, seeking to thwart economic progress and prosperity.

- The environmental crises we face today are the direct result of the "dominion" dogma taught for centuries based on Genesis 1. Christians have taught the idea of subduing the planet. Well they've *subdued* it all right.

- The whole environmental debate is overblown. The Bible says it's all going to burn up anyway. The Church has more important concerns to occupy its attention.

- The earth is our "Sacred Mother," the source of life for all species, and as such must be protected.

- The "going green" movement in business and government is just a sham designed to exercise undue control and increase profits.

It's not hard to recognize that the viewpoints represented above are not only all over the map, but they also conflict with one another radically. They can't all be right. Choices have to be made. So if I put you in front of a microphone and camera to broadcast to the world, what would you be willing to declare as your convictions about the environment? What's true? What's false? What's right? How should we live, and why?

And your answer would be . . .?

Well, here's a confession. Until recently my thinking about the environment has not been very specific. I know God made the earth, I recycle, and I keep my thermostat high during the hot months and low during the cold ones. But I would have to admit I was going along with the herd, doing what everyone else seemed to be doing. And I didn't always know exactly why.

In preparation for this chapter, I had to ask myself a serious question that I trust you are ready to ponder with me: "How, as a follower of Jesus Christ, do I need to think, and act, and respond with regard to the environment?"

Starting with God

Maybe the best place to start, other than all those heated views above, is to gain a big-picture perspective by finding out what God says about the environment. I mean, what does the Bible actually teach about the world in which we live? Once we have God's position before us, we can look at the leading world-based opinions and discover how much of the truth they represent.

I'm a little ashamed to say I've never done a study of Scripture with the purpose of highlighting Biblical insights on the environment. It has come up in a peripheral way over the years, like when I've pondered the way creation declares the glory of God (Psalm 19), but the planet itself hasn't been a central concern of mine.

I'm happy to say that lack of awareness is behind me. I have identified six specific precepts the Bible makes about the environment and our responsibility to it. Let's examine these six claims, match them up with the current views they most echo or challenge, and nail down the Biblical implications from them.

Precept 1: The earth belongs to God.

God owns the earth as an artist owns his art. The world is His property—He created it. This is foundational to everything the

Bible says about the world and our role in it. Psalm 24:1–2 says, "The earth is the LORD's, and everything in it, the world, and all who live in it, for he founded it on the seas, and established it on the waters."

We find the same thought in Psalm 89:11: "The heavens are yours, and yours also the earth; you founded the world and all that is in it." And not just the physical world, but its inhabitants belong to God: "Now if you obey me fully and keep my covenant, then out of all nations you will be my treasured possession. Although the whole earth is mine" (Exod. 19:5). In other words, we're *all* God's possession but He chose a people (Israel) to be His "treasured possession." Whatever we do to the earth and with the earth, we must be aware that we are handling what belongs to God.

The implication of God's ownership creates a duty for us to honor His creation. The very first thing we read in the Bible is, "In the beginning God created the heavens and the earth" (Gen. 1:1). Scripture goes on to describe the creation process. While He was creating the world, God repeatedly declared, "It is good. It is good!" Later, when He made the pinnacle of creation, which is you and me, He said, "It's *very* good."

So how do you honor God? He's the greatest artist and the greatest architect—infinite, all-wise, all-powerful, and all-knowing. One of the great ways we can honor Him is by respecting what He has made. We study what He has made. And we give Him honor, credit, and praise for the beauty and the provision in all He has made for us.

The earth is valuable, precious, irreplaceable, and—here's a word we don't use often enough referring to the earth—sacred. It's not just a piece of land. It's not just air to breathe. God made it. It's sacred.

A trite illustration brought this truth into focus for me. Early in our marriage I was working part-time for a wealthy gentleman. Theresa and I were "seminary poor" at that time, but we had planned a little getaway weekend.

My boss knew what we were doing, and the day I was going to leave, he pulled me aside and said, "Hey, Chip! I have a little gift to help you really enjoy your time." He held out and dropped into my hands the keys to his brand new Datsun 280Z, probably the hottest sports car going at the time. I glanced over at the parking lot where that silver streak of stylish machine was parked.

My first thought was, *If I wreck that car I'll die. It's my boss's pride and joy.* Then I thought, *I probably should test drive it, just to make sure it's going to be okay for me and my wife on this trip.* It was like being in the cockpit of a jet airplane. I jammed the accelerator a few times. That's when I said, "This is way too much fun!"

> **The earth is valuable, precious, irreplaceable, and—here's a word we don't use often enough referring to the earth—sacred.**

But I have to admit I was a little nervous during the trip. When we got to the hotel, all I could think about was parking the car where it wouldn't get "dinged" by someone else's door. And talk about defensive driving!

Here's my point: My boss entrusted me with something precious for our pleasure, but I felt a tremendous weight of responsibility to not only enjoy it but to not mess it up. How much more should we consider the planet God has entrusted to you and me?

Biblical Implication = We are to honor God's creation.
Genesis 1:1

Precept 2: God appointed humankind with dominion over the earth.

Psalm 115:16 says, "The highest heavens belong to the LORD, but the earth he has given to mankind." Note the two words "belong" and "given." God has basically said, "I've created this magnificent planet and I've entrusted it to the human race." What does that mean?

Here's the implication: we are the earth's vice-regents. We are the caretakers, managers, and stewards of creation. God says, "I've created all this but I'm putting you in charge."

The Scripture records the "hand-off" to humans in Genesis 1:28: "God blessed them and said to them, 'Be fruitful and increase in number; fill the earth and subdue it. Rule over the fish in the sea and the birds in the sky and over every living creature that moves on the ground.'" The two key words for our discussion are "subdue" and "rule." The Hebrew words are very strong and are used elsewhere to describe absolute control. God says, "You are fully in charge on My behalf."

God's words convey a real sense of authority and power. The blessing implies, "Do well with this earth—cultivate it; develop it; grow it; tame it." Managing it with excellence and creativity is the idea.

But we've got a problem. Some have taken those strong words of responsibility out of context. They have twisted this blessing to mean we can do with the earth whatever we please. The reasoning goes like this: "It's made for us and we can treat it any way we want to meet our needs." We have emphasized the "subdue and rule" portion of the text while conveniently losing sight of the context of stewardship for God's glory and God's purposes—*not* selfish ends.

Later, in Genesis 2:15, God provides a little more detail about the duties He has in mind for us. "The Lord God took the man and put him in the Garden of Eden to work it and take care of it," or literally, to cultivate and manage it.

God gave us this huge opportunity, this precious possession, and the responsibility to care for it the way He would care for it. Ruling and stewardship always go together when it comes to the environment.

Ruling and stewardship always go together when it comes to the environment.

Shortly after Theresa and I were married, we packed up everything we owned in a Ryder truck, hitched our car to the back bumper, and moved to Texas to attend seminary.

At the time we had seven hundred dollars to our names. We had no place to live, and I did not have a job. Our first breakthrough came when a missionary in Dallas informed us they were going to be out of the country for eight weeks. "You can put all your stuff in our garage and live in our house while we're gone." He graciously gave us complete dominion over his house. "You can have anything in our refrigerator.

We have some fruit trees in the back and you can help yourselves. My car is there, and if you need to use it, it's yours."

I was given this huge opportunity. Living in a free house was fun and gave me time to work a number of part-time jobs to pay for school. We eventually found a place to live, and it all worked out well.

However, during that time, in order to get all of our stuff in his garage, I had to move his car and park it at an angle on the side of the road. Being new to Texas, we were not accustomed to the weather conditions. So for six weeks his vehicle didn't move while it slowly baked under the 100 degree heat of the Texas sun. When I went to drive it back into the garage, I discovered that the sun focused through the window had melted the control switch of the windshield wipers.

I realized immediately the repair was going to cost us more than we had. We were already scraping the bottom of the barrel to pay the deposit fee on our apartment. But I also knew I couldn't leave the car damaged. Broke, desperate, and without a clue how to fix it . . . I prayed.

Then a miracle occurred. It's one of the early miracles of my life. I'm the last person you want doing mechanical work on your car. But I managed to get the part off the steering column, took the melted mess to a junkyard, and discovered God had providentially arranged the exact same model with the part I needed to be there. I even managed to put the new part back on the car—and it worked! Maybe not a big deal to you, but it was a crossing-of-the-Red-Sea moment for me.

Here's my takeaway from that experience: it never entered my mind that I could leave his car or anything else he had entrusted to me in worse condition than it was when he gave it to me.

Someone taught me early in my journey, "A disciple always leaves things better than he found them." We need to recognize how our heavenly Father feels and thinks about this planet He placed under our dominion. We have power to subdue but not abuse God's possession. We are to cultivate and care for it because we are vice-regents over the earth.

Biblical Implication = We are the earth's vice-regents.
Genesis 1:28; 2:15

Precept 3: The earth has intrinsic value and reflects the character and beauty of the Creator.

The earth not only has intrinsic value, but it also reflects the character and beauty of the Creator. Words to highlight in that statement are "character" and "beauty." Scripture says in Psalm 19:1–2, "The heavens declare the glory of God; the skies proclaim the work of his hands. Day after day they pour forth speech; night after night they reveal knowledge." Look at the verbs of communication in that verse: *declare, proclaim, pour forth,* and *reveal.* God intends His creation to announce and communicate who He is and what He is like.

Yes, the earth is a gift from God with oxygen, plants, four-footed creatures that can become food, and creatures you can put heavy weight on so you don't have to carry it. Creatures you can train to pull a plow through the earth in preparation for planting.

God told us, "Subdue, develop, use your mind, be a co-creator." But we started out as just gatherers and hunters. Later we began to learn about seeds and then we planted crops. We created herds of animals and learned about breeding and harvesting products like milk from livestock.

The same God who made us capable of harvesting all the bounty held by the earth also made us capable of doing it in a way that does not harm the environment.

Eventually we used our minds to learn how to develop and use technology to remove materials from the earth that are useful and valuable, like various metals. God knew when He created all of this that there were vast deposits of fossil fuels beneath the surface of the earth. He also knew that we would have the ability to extract them as we learned more and continued to develop technology.

But the same God who made us capable of harvesting all the bounty held by the earth also made us capable of doing it in a way that does not harm the environment. He created it with great beauty, and our task is to preserve that beauty as much as possible.

God says, "I made My world in a way that reveals My character and My beauty. I didn't have to have over three hundred kinds of beetles. I didn't have to make billions of galaxies. The Alps don't have to be that beautiful. The Grand Canyon doesn't have to be that breathtaking. I didn't have to make an ecosystem that is so delicate and so amazingly interdependent that I charged insect life with the duties of pollination to ensure your success in raising crops.

All of those countless marvels I've created reflect that I'm the all-wise God who wields power and produces beauty everywhere."

The implication for us as stewards is that we're free to explore but not exploit. We can enjoy but not worship the earth. Some of us and our children need to spend more time *in* the environment! Living in isolation from nature is not healthy for us, and it's not the way God designed us!

The created order and the wonders of nature can not only impress us, but they can comfort and draw us into a deeper appreciation of God Himself. The apostle Paul was getting to the heart of things when he wrote, "What may be known about God is plain to them, because God has made it plain to them. For since the creation of the world God's invisible qualities—his eternal power and divine nature—have been clearly seen, being understood from what has been made, so that people are without excuse" (Rom. 1:19–20).

There's a part of the power, and the wisdom, and the beauty of God's majesty that soaks into your soul through nature. He speaks through His Word, but He also speaks through nature. He speaks to your heart. The impact of seeing the Grand Canyon or the night sky can give you an overwhelming sense that the God who created all those stars and billions of galaxies really does have the power to restore a broken marriage, help you get a job, and give you the grace to forgive someone who betrayed or abused you.

The world is made to teach us, to renew us. As I see the changing of the seasons, and how things die and come back to life, I'm reminded that in times of failure and disappointment, God is trying to tell me there are seasons of winter and death, but there's new life in spring. Nature gets my attention, but the intent is to point beyond itself. As amazing as the wonders of creation are, they can never replace the wonder of the Creator.

But there is potential danger in developing an appreciation of the environment. We can get so involved in nature that we begin to worship it. This error in worship goes back to the beginning of time. The passage from Romans 1 mentioned above comes from a longer discussion by the apostle Paul regarding the moral and spiritual crisis facing humanity.

There's no real mystery to the fact that places of spectacular natural beauty like Santa Cruz, California; Sedona, Arizona; and Boulder, Colorado, to mention just a few, become centers for new age, nature worship. People who begin to worship the creation soon lose sight of the Creator. But when you begin to focus on the Creator and see His creation as an amazing example of what He can do, you get an accurate picture of His greatness, His wisdom, His love, and His beauty.

Again, when Paul said, "What may be known about God is plain to them" (Rom. 1:19), he was highlighting the fact that God has not left us clueless about Himself. How? What is so plain about God? The apostle continued, "Since the creation of the world God's invisible qualities—his eternal power and divine nature—have been clearly seen, being understood from that which has been made, so that people are without excuse." Looking at nature should never make us think, *This is powerful and divine*, but it should provoke us to conclude, *This is certainly made by Someone awesomely powerful and divine!*

C. S. Lewis pointed out that people who claim no belief in God have to be on their guard all the time. In one way or another we assume God's existence even when we don't really want to. I chuckled over a recent comment someone made about interacting with atheists: "They categorically deny the existence of God but also insist on talking about how angry they are with Him." The problem people have isn't with evidence for God. It goes deeper. Romans 1:21 continues, "For although they knew God, they neither glorified him as God nor gave thanks to him, but their thinking became futile and their foolish hearts were darkened."

People may say, "I can't believe in God," but what they mean is, "I refuse to believe in God despite the evidence." Among such people the choice to worship nature itself is an escape from the reality of worshiping the One who created it all.

Meanwhile God says, "Enjoy, but don't worship it." The earth is not your mother. The earth is a created, beautiful gift from your heavenly Father, to reveal His character and to provide for you.

> **Biblical Implication = We must explore, not exploit;
> enjoy, not worship, the earth.** Romans 1:19–21

Precept 4: Humanity is placed in the middle of the created hierarchy and is uniquely responsible to God above and for the animals, plants, and resources below.

To understand this statement, let's focus on the terms "hierarchy" and "uniquely responsible." We have already seen that when God made the universe and the earth, He said, "It's good." He said the same about the vegetable and animal part of creation. But He reserved the term "very good" for the moment when He created the human race. He put Adam in the middle of the Garden of Eden and in the middle of His created order for a purpose.

A little lower than the Creator, there is mankind, made in His image, unlike any animal or any plant. We can think, feel, and reason. We were made for a relationship with Him and responsibility to Him. Then there are animals, the animate, living things God made with breath and purpose. And there are inanimate things like plants and trees and rocks. And right in the middle of that are you and me, humankind.

Our place in the created order means we have a responsibility and a stewardship role upward to our Creator, and we have a responsibility downward to treat animals and plants and the rest of the creation with this delicate balance of using it for our good (productivity) and also preservation and restoration.

Psalm 8 captures our unique placement in creation: "When I consider your heavens, the work of your fingers, the moon and the stars, which you have set in place" (v. 3). The psalmist is doing exactly what nature was designed to make us do—ponder the awesomeness of God. "What is mankind that you are mindful of them, human beings that you care for them? You have made them a little lower than the angels and crowned them with glory and honor" (vv. 4–5).

Notice next the role we have in the environment: "You made them rulers over the works of your hands; you put everything under their feet: all flocks and herds, and the animals of the wild, the birds in the sky, and the fish in the sea, all that swim the paths of the seas" (vv. 6–7). That reads like a job description designed by the Creator for us.

One of the implications of our role is that all living things have value, but not all living things have equal value. The earth is not

God. It is not our mother. It is a created thing. In like manner whales and human babies do not have equal value. Yet when we think wrongly about the environment, we kill babies and save whales. Think of it. That's a theological issue flowing directly out of our stewardship role profoundly affected by our exaltation of the creation over the Creator's clear priority and hierarchy within creation.

Should we save whales? Absolutely. But when part of the environmental community declares that your dog or cat or a lizard has the same intrinsic rights (or more) as you do because they are, like you, just part of the living species, they are in error. Our responsibility toward other humans can't be sacrificed on the altar of stewardship for nature. God calls us to be good stewards of nature, but animals don't have the same intrinsic rights as humans. Instead, we are to use—not abuse—animals, plants, and resources to glorify God.

We as Christians have been some of the slowest to be responsible in the areas of stewardship of the environment and concern for it.

The Bible is so amazingly balanced. Proverbs 12:10–11 tells us, "The righteous care for the needs of their animals, but the kindest acts of the wicked are cruel. Those who work their land will have abundant food, but those who chase fantasies have no sense." Scripture is very clear about the responsibilities and consequences reflected in how we treat animals and the earth. But we as Christians have been some of the slowest to be responsible in the areas of stewardship of the environment and concern for it. We need to own our waste, ignorance, and lack of care and concern for the world God entrusted to us.

When I was a kid, Lake Erie became so contaminated that no living thing could survive in it. The entire lake was declared dead. Decades of pollutants and abuse had left behind a toxic mix. At the heart of pollution are greed, ignorance, and carelessness. The attitude and values that lead to these can be summarized this way: "We don't need to care about other people. We're not responsible for the planet. And we don't need to consider long-term implications." The motivation that drives it? "What can we get now? How much can we get? How fast can we do it?"

Those attitudes and objectives always lead to abuse and exploitation.

On the other hand, God's Word says very clearly, "You should be productive. Take things out of the ground wisely. There's energy to be had. That's why I put it there." But our track record has been very poor since the Industrial Revolution. Strip mining, clear-cutting, and other short-term, high-result approaches have created a bumper crop of environmental shame sites. Many believers have either ignored our responsibilities or hoped it would all go away. We have often unfairly viewed environmentalists as "one size fits all" radicals or extremists.

The Bible has quite a bit to say about our role. God Himself honors efforts people make to treat His world responsibly. The experts said it would take fifty to a hundred years for any life to be regenerated in Lake Erie. Yet five to ten years after the pollutants stopped, fish were flourishing again. The Creator built into His world amazing recovery capabilities, if we will only give them a chance. The staggering oil spill in the Gulf of Mexico several years ago seemed to foreshadow a disaster all along the southern coast. Yes, it took a huge effort on the part of humans, but we can't ignore the amazing cooperation from God and His creative genius. All the organisms and natural capacities for self-cleaning have surpassed what we could have done on our own.

The warnings about care and the efforts not to abuse the earth while we are exploring and enjoying its benefits need to be heard and heeded by all of us.

> **Biblical Implication = We are to use, not abuse, animals, plants, and resources for the glory of God.**
> *Psalm 8:3–8*

Precept 5: God commands environmental stewardship to protect the land, animals, and vegetation for the common good.

As Creator, God says, "Yes, mankind, you're above it. You are the pinnacle of my creation. But I own it, and you're a steward who has been given dominion, authority, and responsibility. Don't worship it. Enjoy it. Steward it well. You have a responsibility to care for the land, the animals, and the vegetation."

To which you might ask, "Where does God say that?"

All the way back in the Old Testament, when God was preparing the Israelites to be a great nation, He put them into a training regimen. He liberated them, a group of slaves out of Egypt, by demonstrating His complete sovereignty over the nature-gods that surrounded them. Each of the ten plagues in Exodus was a polemic against one of the gods of Egypt. From threatening the Nile, which is still the "lifeblood" of the region, to the darkening of the sun, God humiliated the "gods" of Egypt and displayed their impotence against Him.

God brought the Israelites to Sinai and continued to reveal who He is. God gave them laws about His holiness in Leviticus. And much of the Pentateuch, written during the Exodus years, is saying to Israel, "This is the kind of nation I want You to be . . ." He began giving them rules and decrees, assuring them that His instructions would allow them to become a nation that would draw the attention of other nations to God. Obedience would preserve them and cause their nation to prosper like no other.

We read those laws centuries later and are astounded by God's wisdom. His people didn't know about bacteria. But God gave them ceremonial laws about washing their hands, reducing the spread of many of the common diseases of the day. As one representative from Compassion International told me, 80 percent of all sickness could be eliminated worldwide with soap and fresh water. The Israelites didn't know about the unusually high blood clotting capacity on the eighth day after birth (confirmed by scientific research), but they had God's command to circumcise their sons on the eighth day.[1]

They didn't know anything about the depletion of nitrates and other nutrients from the soil caused by repeatedly planting the same crops. Yet in Leviticus 25, before they were even in the Promised Land, God told them, "After every sixth year, leave the land fallow on the seventh."

God didn't want His land treated like an expendable commodity. So He declared that every fiftieth year would be a Year of Jubilee, when all the land leased or sold to others would return to its ancestral owners. Families were to be good stewards of their heritage. God knew that with no limitations on the transfer and ownership of property, the rich get richer and the poor get poorer.

So He ordered, "Every fifty years we're going to reboot the system." If a family owned land, it could never be sold permanently. Loans, mortgages, land use, and servanthood were to be carried out under the fifty-year rule. And God's reason was, "You and the land belong to Me."

In addition to addressing the land, God gives very specific instruction about how animals are to be treated in Deuteronomy 25:4. "Do not muzzle an ox while it is treading out the grain." God cares about the animals, and we are commanded to treat them well. In Deuteronomy 20:19 He instructs the nation when in battle and besieging a city, "Do not destroy its trees . . . because you can eat their fruit." Isn't it amazing that God would give rules and provisions for what we assume was a very low technology group of people, to preserve animals, the soil, and the ecologic system?

Here's the implication of God's guidelines: consumption and productivity must be governed by the boundaries of conservation.

Are we going to be consumers? Of course we are. Do we need to be productive? Yes! But fruitfulness and productivity must be practiced with wisdom, responsibility, and conservation.

Our track record on caring for the air we breathe, the water we drink, and the plants we consume has lacked Biblical stewardship. As long as our greed and speed urge us always to produce more in a short amount of time, to get more money, we will violate God's clear directives and destroy the earth in the process.

I remember going to visit my grandparents as a ten-year-old for a week by myself. I was a pretty adventuresome kid and, frankly, hanging out with Grandma and Grandpa was pretty boring after about two days. They lived in a little brick house backed up to a very steep hill in West Virginia. It seemed like a mountain begging to be climbed. My interest was increased when my grandmother said, "Don't go up there."

I admit that didn't stop me. I will never forget getting up to the very top and taking my first look at the land beyond. What I saw looked like a bad science fiction movie, where a nuclear blast had occurred.

At the time I didn't know anything about strip mining, but I sensed something terribly wrong had gone on there. All I could see were miles of sandy, brownish color, big rocks, no trees, and no vegetation. There were no animals. It was like seeing the surface of the moon. The land was raped. The process was fast and people made money, but it destroyed every living thing. Let me be very clear: it is un-Christian to treat the earth in this way.

But a reaction to past practices can swing the pendulum too far in the other direction. Today, in California, we have thousands of farmers out of work, crops dying in the fields, and millions of lives impacted because a salamander (or other creature) is deemed to be endangered. Irrigation for farmland has been denied to preserve the salamander. This salamander is very important, but we need water to grow crops, not simply for California but for the whole nation. There will always be dynamic tension and trade-offs between the needs of people and the preservation of the earth. What is needed is wisdom and discernment in view of both short-term needs and long-term implications.

These aren't hypothetical situations. We have people on one side who are so environmentally sensitive that every species is given absolute veto power over the needs of people. Technology needs to be harnessed with wisdom and balance. But human ingenuity can often be applied to these problems in a way that is beneficial to both sides. The salamander gets its habitat and the resources can be accessed.

Clearly we Christians need a Biblical view of the environment. Because there are conflicting interests and the reality of sin in the world, there is going to be tension in resolving how to live well in the world. But if I understand that the earth belongs to God, that I've been given responsible dominion, that God has instructed us to appreciate and enjoy the earth but not worship it, that each of us is going to give an account for our work as a steward of creation, and that I am free to use the earth but never abuse it, then these truths create a lens through which I can begin to see how to honor the planet and make sure people's needs are met.

Biblical Implication = Consumption and productivity must be governed by the boundaries of conservation.
Leviticus 25:1–12, 23

Precept 6: Christ's redemptive work includes the earth.

In Romans 8:19–21, creation is personified as looking forward to and yearning for the day when redemption is going to occur. The passage says:

For the creation waits in eager expectation for the children of God to be revealed. For the creation was subjected to frustration, not by its own choice, but by the will of the one who subjected it, in hope that the creation itself will be liberated from its bondage to decay and brought into the freedom and glory of the children of God.

This passage is in sharp contrast to the warped theology of some who say, "It's all going to burn anyway, so why bother with the earth or the environment?" In fact, comments like the above have cast Christianity in a very negative light among those who take our environment seriously. Worse yet, the Church in large measure has seemed ignorant of God's Word concerning the importance of the earth now and in the future.

According to this text in Romans, the fall of man (when sin entered the world) had devastating implications not only for mankind in their relationship to God and with one another, but also for the creation. Prior to man's rebellion, the creation knew nothing of tornados, tsunamis, and earthquakes. The earth "was subjected to frustration, not by its own choice" (Rom. 8:20).

In other words, our sin had a direct impact on the environment. Just as our lives, relationships, and bodies reflect the corruption and evidence of death caused by sin, so does the creation.

Yet just as sin impacted creation, back at the fall, so Christ's work of redemption impacted creation at the cross. When Jesus died and rose again from the dead, He paid the purchase price for sin. Jesus bought us out of the slave market of sin by His own blood (Mark 10:45). This work of Christ is the basis of salvation for all who will turn from their sin and receive this free gift of forgiveness and new life.

What many don't realize is that this act of redemption not only positioned humans to be restored to God and one another; it also means He will one day restore the earth to His original plan. The creation will be "liberated from its bondage to decay and brought into the freedom and glory of the children of God" (Rom. 8:21). The implication from this passage is obvious: we should treat the earth with the same priority God does.

The fact is that the earth matters to God and He wants it to matter to us. He longs for us to see His overarching plan and grace to restore the created order. We are to participate in that plan with wisdom and balance in a fallen world.

Perhaps nothing has reoriented my view of the earth's value and importance to God like my recent study of heaven. In Isaiah 65:17 and Revelation 21:1–4 we get a very specific picture of God's eternal plan and environment for those who by faith have received forgiveness and new life.

> See, I will create new heavens and a new earth. The former things will not be remembered, nor will they come to mind. (Isa. 65:17)

> Then I saw "a new heaven and a new earth," for the first heaven and the first earth had passed away, and there was no longer any sea. I saw the Holy City, the new Jerusalem, coming down out of heaven from God, prepared as a bride beautifully dressed for her husband. And I heard a loud voice from the throne saying, "Look! God's dwelling place is now among the people, and he will dwell with them. They will be his people, and God himself will be with them and be their God. He will wipe every tear from their eyes. There will be no more death or mourning or crying or pain, for the old order of things has passed away." (Rev. 21:1–4)

The new heaven and the new earth will be just like Eden was supposed to be. God's original environment was to have fellowship with His people on a perfect earth with plants, trees, rivers, and animals. We were to manage it, be vice-regents with Him, build, grow, develop, and cultivate it in perfect relationship with Him and one another.

God's agenda for His vice-regents here on earth today is to be a part of restoring the earth, whenever possible.

Well, the eternal state will be such a place. Yes, the moment we die as believers, we are immediately ushered into the presence of Christ in what theologians call the intermediate state. And yes, Christ will come back and judge the earth, the nations, Satan, his angels, and all humankind at the Great White Throne (Revelation 20). But the eternal state (heaven as we call it) will not be some immaterial, eternal state. Our eternity will not be spent playing harps or participating in one eternal church service.

Note, carefully, a new heaven and a *new earth* will be our future. We will share Jesus's likeness in resurrected bodies, worship, and enjoy God on a real earth with real culture, real jobs, music, animals, trees, rivers, and life as He always intended it to be.

God's future new earth will be amazing! Just like we are changing and being conformed progressively to the image of Christ, so God's agenda for His vice-regents here on earth today is to be a part of restoring the earth, whenever possible. As followers of Jesus, we have a moral and spiritual responsibility to care for the environment.

Biblical Implication = We must treat the earth with the same priority God does. Revelation 21:1–4

Living It Out

Before we talk specifically about living out these five statements from Scripture, I invite you to take just a moment and flip back through the pages to review them.

I think the great majority of Christians have no idea how much God has said about the environment and how seriously He takes it. We all have blind spots, and this certainly seems to be one for many of us. So, with that said, how do we embrace practically what God tells us when it comes to caring for this earth of His?

First, I think we need to begin with eight verifiable issues on which we can all agree. Certainly there are diverse opinions and a wide range of "research" from opposing views on global warming and other controversial issues; but what if rather than *arguing* we all committed to acting on these issues:

1. Clean air
2. Clean water
3. Balanced land use
4. Preservation of beauty
5. Productivity and progress with constraints for conservation
6. Waste minimization
7. Limits for nonbiodegradable plastics
8. Recycling

Can you imagine the difference the Church could make all around the world if we did nothing more than commit to caring for God's planet by championing these eight priorities? Our tendency is to blame or criticize others or think that only "major" reforms can make a difference. But tens of millions of Christians recycling consistently, minimizing waste, and making informed decisions would drastically "move the needle" toward what God desires for this earth.

Second, we would be less than honest if we didn't identify the root causes of our poor environmental stewardship. We all have to take responsibility, and that only happens when we are honest. There may be more, but I see these three root causes as:

1. Greed
2. Ignorance
3. Carelessness

Greed may sound like a strong word, but it's what drives our "I want it convenient, I want it fast, and I want it efficiently packaged" mentality of consumption. We've created a fast-paced, over-consuming culture of convenience that produces huge amounts of waste, packaging that is not biodegradable, and food that is not nutritious.

Our ignorance is demonstrated by how little we teach on environmental issues in the Church. When I taught this material at the church I pastor, I asked, "How many of you have ever heard a message on God's concern for the earth or the environment?" Only a handful of people raised their hand in a church of several thousand.

Carelessness, unfortunately, seems to go hand in hand with abundance. We rarely think of conserving things that we unconsciously perceive as unlimited. We intellectually know water and energy are limited and precious, but when we turn on the faucet, we take for granted that we have all we want or need. When it gets hot or cold, we carelessly set the thermostat on what produces the "greatest comfort," not on what would be the wisest use. So let's get very specific on how to become better stewards of this precious place called Earth.

Four Ways to Care for the Earth

Here are four practical steps to help you get started as a Christ-follower who wants to honor God with how you treat the environment. I call them the Four E's.

1. *Explore*—Get outside. Go to the park, take a walk, get beyond the city lights, and take a long look at all those stars in the sky. If you're close, go to the ocean, mountains, national parks, or state nature preserves. Commit to restoring your childlike wonder and awe of the beauty and majesty of God's creation.

2. *Educate*—Learn about nature, the solar system, the galaxy, and the amazing world beneath the sea. Read an article about whales, migration, or bees, or watch the Discovery Channel with your kids. Detach from the electronic world of mobile devices, computers, and fluorescent lights. You will never guard and protect what you don't appreciate.

3. *Engage*—Choose to do something. Recycle even if your town doesn't. Conserve water, heat, and energy as an offering to God, not a commitment to "go green" or to be politically correct. Take some steps that might not save the planet but that will remind you to be a steward and not a consumer. For example, I had the habit of letting the water run while

I shaved in the morning. It was a careless habit that has wasted more gallons of water in the last four decades than I can admit. While doing this study, God convicted me. Is it a big deal? Maybe not. Will it transform the world's water supply? No. But I now have a daily reminder and practice that has me reorienting my greed, ignorance, and carelessness toward conservation and stewardship. What might you do?

4. *Empower*—Finally, consider taking a step toward those who are most vocal and most committed to the environment. Consider going to an Earth Day celebration and learning from those who may be a "little over the top" or even "radical" from your perspective. Consider being a bold representative of Jesus Christ by action and words to communicate that you want to help preserve this planet. Not because it is your "mother" or because it's "godlike," but because it is "your Father's world." What if the environmental community found honest, noncritical followers of Jesus who said, "We'd like to help. What can we learn from you?"

What would happen if we were open and chose to embrace others who share a common concern for the earth? Will there be disagreements and the need for balance? Quite definitely! But what might God do if the most environmentally sensitive people on the face of the earth were Christians?

I think we might see a lot of people open their ears and heart to not just the environment but to the One who made it.

CHAPTER 7
POLITICS
WHAT'S THE ROLE OF THE CHURCH?

Render to Caesar the things that are Caesar's;
and to God the things that are God's.

Matthew 22:21 NASB
Jesus of Nazareth

Many years ago, after preaching about the sanctity of human life, I received a letter from a woman that had to be, at the time, the most scathing letter in my young pastoral career. Right out of the gate she said, "I can't believe you were talking about politics in the Church! Why don't you preachers keep your noses in the Bible and out of politics? When I come to church, this is not what I want to hear! You should be excommunicated from ministry! You shouldn't even be a pastor! It's the worst, most horrific . . ." And on and on and on it went.

I remember leaning back thinking, *Oh my lands! A moral issue becomes political and I teach right out of the Bible about how God cherished us, even while in our mother's womb [Psalm 139], and this is what I get?*

Later I learned that she didn't even attend the service. She heard about the sermon from a friend, and from her perspective this was undoubtedly a political issue. She basically said to me, "How could you say you love God and talk about that in church?" even though it was a core, Biblical, moral issue.

On the other hand, I've been greeted in the hallways of the church, in the mall, or even in my office with people who have red faces and bulging veins, who scream three inches from my face, "You don't understand! If you don't take a stand right now on this issue [or support this candidate or tell people how to vote], America's going to hell! It's time for the Church to say it like it is from the pulpit and step up!" What these people are saying to me is, "How can you say you love God and not take a stand on political issues in the Church?"

Well, I have to tell you that, in all my years as a pastor, I have found few issues that are so divisive, that cut so deep, that anger so many, or that have more Christians at odds with one another than the issue of the Church and politics. And when you dive into this subject, you find some people who think there should be no church involvement (often called "separatists") and others who think there should be complete involvement ("activists").

My goal in this chapter is to bring a little light to this issue instead of pouring gasoline on the fire. And in so doing I hope we can unpack some presuppositions together and better understand why people sincerely and passionately think the way they do.

The Separatist

Their Premise

How can you love God, yet talk about politics in the Church?

Their Position

Any subject that is political, directly or indirectly, should never be talked about from the pulpit.

Their Presuppositions

Like the woman who wrote the scathing letter, some people view politics as "off limits" in a church setting. I've observed three presuppositions that are behind this type of thinking.

First is a clear distinction between what's "sacred" and what's "secular." Faith is a private spiritual relationship where you share sacred moments with God. The world, politics, and everything in between are secular. Some believe these two should never mix and Christian involvement in government should be at an absolute minimum.

Second is a sincere but confused understanding of the difference between a "pluralistic" society versus "pluralism." (See chapter 1 for an explanation of the roots of pluralism in our society.) A pluralistic society believes that we have the right to champion our ideas. We can debate and vote on ideas, but the best ones and the truth will win out. America has loosely followed this model throughout its history. Recently our society has been leaning more and more toward pluralism. That is, every idea has equal weight and value. So for you to say that one idea or position is superior to another is viewed as intolerant.

Third, some believe all government is corrupt. They might tell you, "There's been too much talk and no action. It doesn't matter who I vote for, or if I even vote, because it won't make a difference anyway." This group is what I call "functional separatists." They're disillusioned and completely disengaged.

The Activist

Their Premise

How can you love God and *not* take a stand on political issues in the Church?

Their Position

The Church is a tool in the hand of God to turn the secular culture back to Him. They look to the Church to exercise its voice and actively support candidates, issues, and laws that would bring about an alignment between our government, our culture, and Biblical values.

Their Presuppositions

I've observed three presuppositions behind this point of view.

First, America has a special, covenant relationship with God. This isn't your typical "Biblical worldview in common" type of argument. This position views America's relationship with God not unlike God's covenant relationship with Israel. In this view the goal of the Church is to bring America back to God, and what better way than to be an instrument in God's hand to do just that?

Second, moral and cultural change is the primary mandate of the Church. Basically, by using the political process, the Church's main focus should be on changing the culture, laws, and people so they reflect Biblical values. These people see the Church as a "bully pulpit" and its purpose to achieve Biblical values and corresponding laws largely through the political process.

Third, the Church gathered (or church as a corporate institution) and each "individual Christian" should have the same calling. That is, whatever we do when we're gathered together as a corporate church body, or as an official position, this calling is the same in the life of each follower of Christ.

Some of you may be thinking, "I definitely believe that" or "What's wrong if I believe that?" And still others may be thinking, "Gee, I guess I never really thought about it that way." Please remember there are a lot of opinions out there about what we've just discussed.

Before we start arguing about whether we, in church, should interview political candidates, keep our noses out of the political arena, or have voting guides available, let's take a step back. Let's suspend our strong emotions and get a clear view of what the Bible says about this issue. What does Scripture specifically teach about the role of the Church? When I say the Church, I mean the responsibility of the corporate entity, the Church gathered, and not individual believers. And finally, what does the Bible say about the Church and politics, the role of the government, and our role as individual believers?

The Bible's Absolutes

How can we navigate through the maze of the "Church and politics" conflict?

Scripture does not offer a simple solution like "1 Politics 1:9," but it does provide *four biblical absolutes* to build a theological framework in which we can think clearly about the Church and politics. With these absolutes we will be able to develop some timeless principles to evaluate the separatist and activist positions.

Absolute 1: There are two kingdoms in conflict.

Our first Biblical absolute comes from the very lips of Jesus. He has been in ministry for around three years and his popularity and messages threaten the Jewish leaders. They are afraid that if they let Jesus continue to preach, the Roman Empire or the multitudes will remove them from their positions of power. So they devise a plan, arrest Jesus, and bring Him before Pilate, representing the official government of the day, to have Him crucified. They do this because Jewish law does not allow putting a man to death, but Roman law does. Pilate explains to Jesus that He's been handed over by His own people, and he wants to hear why He deserves a death sentence.

Jesus replies in John 18:36, "My kingdom is not of this world. If it were, my servants would fight to prevent my arrest by the Jewish leaders. But now my kingdom is from another place." Verse 37 records Pilate's response, "You are a king, then!"

Jesus answers in the same verse, "You say that I am a king. In fact, the reason I was born and came into the world is to testify to the truth. Everyone on the side of truth listens to me."

What Jesus is saying is that there's a different kingdom, His kingdom. It isn't of this world and it's rooted in truth. He's pointing out that there are two kingdoms in conflict. First, there is a spiritual, eternal kingdom that Jesus—the Messiah, the Son of God—came to earth to reveal and establish through all those who believe. Then there is the temporal, physical kingdom we live in. This sometimes is referred to as the world's system.

So Pilate, frustrated by Jesus's vague and veiled responses, and by the Jews' unwillingness to free Jesus after twice declaring he finds no basis for a charge against Him, replies, "Do you refuse to speak to me? . . . Don't you realize I have the power either to free you or to crucify you?" (John 19:10). Pilate is flat out telling Jesus, "Don't you get it, Jesus? I have all power and authority over your life in this very moment and you have nothing to say?"

We live in two kingdoms, a spiritual kingdom and a physical kingdom. They are at odds with one another, constantly in conflict.

Here's where our first absolute becomes clear. Jesus answered, "You would have no power over me if it were not given to you from above. Therefore, the one who handed me over to you is guilty of a greater sin" (v. 11).

Jesus's ministry, then and now, is building a spiritual kingdom of love and justice that will ultimately consummate when He returns. So until then, we live in two kingdoms, a spiritual kingdom and a physical kingdom. They are at odds with one another, constantly in conflict.

This raises a crucial question. How are we to live in two kingdoms? And a follow-up to that is, How do we maintain our loyalty and values of following Jesus when they are in direct conflict with the values and laws of the country we live in? The answer may surprise you.

Absolute 2: Every believer has dual citizenship.

This brings us to the second absolute of the Church and politics. Every believer has dual citizenship. The apostle Paul writes in Philippians 3:20 that, if we are born-again believers of Jesus Christ, "our citizenship is in heaven."

Jesus models and explains this dual citizenship in Mark 12:13–17. The setting is contentious and heated. The religious leaders are feeling very threatened; so much so that two groups normally at odds relationally and theologically join forces to eliminate Jesus. They are as far right and as far left as you can imagine. But they agree on one thing: they have a common enemy: Jesus. His popularity, His power with the people, His preaching and teaching are in direct opposition to the religious establishment they control, resulting in a plot to discredit and kill Him. We pick up the story in Mark 12:13–15:

> Later they sent some of the Pharisees [right wingers theologically] and Herodians [left wingers theologically] to Jesus to catch him in his words. They came to him and said, "Teacher, we know that you are a man of integrity. You aren't swayed by others, because you pay no attention to who they are; but you teach the way of God in accordance with the truth. Is it right to pay the imperial tax to Caesar or not? Should we pay or shouldn't we?"

The trap has been set. These two groups of religious leaders have devised what they believe is the perfect question to discredit Jesus. Robed in hypocrisy and attempting to appear sincere, they are sitting on the proverbial edge of their seats thinking, "It doesn't matter what He says, we've got Him now!" If He says they should pay Caesar, the Jewish people will be against Him, but if He answers, "No, we shouldn't pay Caesar," He will be defying the Roman government. So whatever He says, they don't care. Their goal is not to receive an honest answer but to neutralize Jesus's power and influence. His answer not only stuns His opponents but provides us with the answer to our question of how to live in two kingdoms in conflict.

> But Jesus knew their hypocrisy. "Why are you trying to trap me?" he asked. "Bring me a denarius and let me look at it." They brought the coin, and he asked them, "Whose image is this? And whose inscription?" "Caesar's," they replied. Then Jesus said to them, "Give back to Caesar what is Caesar's and to God what is God's." (Mark 12:15–17)

The Jewish leaders use the Greek word *didomi* when they ask Jesus about whom they should pay. This word means "Just give something." In His answer, Jesus uses a different word for "pay." He uses *apodidomi*, which means "to fulfill a debt" or "pay off."

So what He's really saying is, "You have an absolute debt or obligation to Caesar and the government, to give whatever they ask. You also have an equal, if not more important obligation to give to God whatever He asks of you." In other words, every believer has dual citizenship.

You are to be faithful in your citizenship in heaven and faithful in your citizenship here on earth with the governmental authority you're under. But how can we be faithful to both when there's such corruption and evil in the world? The answer to that question leads us to Biblical absolute number three.

Absolute 3: Human governments are ordained by God to restrain evil.

During the time the apostle Paul is writing his letter to the Romans, they were facing serious persecution. And the Roman Empire was deeply corrupt. The injustice and brutality were at an all-time high, infanticide was normal, women were bought and sold as property, slavery was widespread, and immorality ran rampant. It was a culture characterized by sexual license and power with abuse—anything you wanted, any way you wanted, and any time you wanted it.

In this setting, Paul teaches this struggling church how to live out their dual citizenship. He gives them and us some clear instructions on how we can live out our faith in the two kingdoms in conflict. He writes in Romans 13:1–3:

> Let everyone be subject to the governing authorities, for there is no authority except that which God has established. The authorities that exist have been established by God. Consequently, whoever rebels against the authority is rebelling against what God has instituted, and those who do so will bring judgment on themselves. For rulers hold no terror for those who do right, but for those who do wrong. Do you want to be free from fear of one in authority? Then do what is right and you will be commended.

Here the apostle Paul, inspired by the Holy Spirit, is defining the role of government. His thesis is that God in His sovereignty has allowed and even placed government authority to fulfill His purposes. He explains that purpose beginning in verse 4: "For the one in authority is God's servant for your good. But if you do wrong, be afraid, for rulers do not bear the sword for no reason. They are God's servants, agents of wrath to bring punishment on the wrongdoer." The application is clear from this passage both then and now. Whether you lived in Rome in the first century as a Christian or live in Communist China or in America under a democracy today, the government is ordained by God to restrain evil.

The role of government according to Scripture is very simple: it's to restrain evil.

He outlines our response to the government in verse 5: "It is necessary to submit to the authorities, not only because of possible punishment but also as a matter of conscience." Paul is putting a box around how we obey God by submitting to the governing authorities, as long as they don't violate His Word.

The government doesn't have the power to change people's hearts; nor is its purpose from God's perspective to transform culture and bring about righteousness. The role of government according to Scripture is very simple: it's to restrain evil.

But if the government doesn't have the power to bring about moral and cultural change resulting in justice, love, equality, and righteousness, then how is that ever going to happen? What the government can't do through *external control*, God will do through His people.

Absolute 4: The Church is ordained by God to make disciples.

The Bible tells us plainly that the Church is ordained by God to make disciples. The Church, the body of Christ, has a very special purpose, and it is to help its constituents live the way Jesus lived, love the way Jesus loved, and become salt and light in an evil and fallen world. The Church is God's agent of righteousness and love. Even in the midst of absolute evil and terrible governments, Christians live out supernatural, winsome, and holy lives. Throughout human history we have seen this played out—from feeding the poor, to building hospitals and orphanages, to caring for lepers, survivors of plagues, and victims of HIV. The Church has made a difference despite all the troubles and ills in society. Followers of Jesus have been at the forefront of bringing moral and cultural change not by external force, but by *internal transformation.*

Followers of Jesus have been at the forefront of bringing moral and cultural change not by external force, but by *internal transformation.*

Matthew 28:18–20 spells out Christ's agenda for His people: "Then Jesus came to them and said, 'All authority in heaven and on earth has been given to me.'" Here's what Jesus wants you and me to do. "Therefore go and make disciples of all nations, baptizing them in the name of the Father and of the Son and of the Holy Spirit, and teaching them to obey everything I commanded you."

And when it gets out of control, when you're afraid, when you think it's impossible, and when you're worn out, He says, "Surely I am with you always, to the very end of the age" (v. 20).

Making disciples is not as complicated as you may think. It's first and foremost about a relationship. It's about how you live. It's about living, by the power of the Holy Spirit, like Jesus in your arena of influence at home, at work, everywhere! It's about permeating the lives of those around you with hope, love, and genuine concern. While modeling righteous values even when it's not popular. You do that by fulfilling your role with the government and submitting. You realize that God in His sovereignty has placed you in a country under a dictatorship, a democracy, a communist regime, or whatever form of government you're under for His purpose. And God says, "In the midst of the corruption, evil, and pain that exists in all governments and societies, I want you to be 'little Christs,' whom I will use to transform lives and laws and cultures from the inside out. Like the leaven that starts small and saturates the whole loaf, I will use my ordinary followers to bring about change and goodness beyond their wildest imaginations."

If you think I'm overstating my case, let me share a story that will help you see how God works. I have a close friend whom I've known for almost twenty years. We have a ton in common. We have the same, exact birthday so we are the same age. We were both discipled by the same parachurch group. And we are both in positions of influence that we never dreamed we would have.

This is a passionate Christ-follower who gets up every morning and reads God's Word. He's hungry for ways to grow his faith. He leads a Bible study, serves in his church, and meets with men to mentor and disciple them. He "gets" two things unequivocally: (1) "I am to follow Jesus personally," and (2) "I'm supposed to help change the world in my sphere of influence." David is Chinese, and after he finished his education in America, he went back to Hong Kong and eventually became the CEO of one of the largest corporations in China.

A little over a year ago, we were having lunch and I asked him, "Tell me, David, how do you do it? I mean, with all the persecution in China, how are you able to live the Christian life and help others grow in their faith?" He looked me right in the eyes and said, "You know, Chip, when Christians live like Christians and we're the very best citizens, it's amazing the favor God gives us with the government."

He said, "I was having lunch with the Minister for Religious Affairs." My jaw dropped. In other words, he was meeting with the person in China who's in charge of anything religious for the entire country. And the Minister for Religious Affairs said, "Look, when you bring all of your accounting and financial people into the major cities for training, you are free to gather in groups of up to one hundred people. You can pray, you can worship, you can invite people and do what you want, but don't get too big and don't get noisy about it. Your firm with its ethics and integrity is what China needs. I'm not opposed to your Christianity; it's actually quite helpful to our society. What we don't want in China is destabilization."

Now, is there persecution of Christians in China? Absolutely. But hear this: the reason this particular group has been given such freedom is because of the lifestyles of the believers in David's firm. They're honest, trustworthy, and exemplary in their work.

What the Chinese government understands is that they can trust the kind of people who work for David's firm.

David continued, "In every province there's a huge growth in home churches, and Christians are positively impacting their communities. The result is prosperity. Christians obeying the government except when told not to read the Bible or pray demonstrates the power of the gospel even in the most adverse circumstances." These Christians are transforming the spiritual and moral climate of their country without destabilizing the government's power.

Governments have the power to restrain evil. They don't have the power, laws don't have the power, and Supreme Court justices don't have the power to create righteousness in people's hearts.

So as believers of Jesus Christ, we live in two kingdoms that are in conflict. We all have dual citizenship, one in heaven and one in our country. The government is ordained to restrain evil and the Church is called to make authentic disciples, resulting in internal transformation of lives, values, and morals.

The government is ordained to restrain evil and the Church is called to make authentic disciples, resulting in internal transformation of lives, values, and morals.

These four Biblical absolutes help us think clearly about the role of the Church, the government, and the individual believer. Now let's tackle the big question.

The Big Question: How Do We Move from a Theological Framework to Specific Application for Daily Living?

If you're like me, the first question you have is, "So how do we put this into practice? How do these four absolutes play out in the Church and in addressing the political issues that we face today?" Let me suggest six Biblical principles that emerge from our study that help us understand and apply the roles and responsibilities of the church, the government, and the individual believer in the political arena. When we clarify the role and responsibility of each, then we can make honest, educated decisions about what the Church should do, what the government should do, and what individual Christians should do.

1. Let the Church be the Church!

The Church's highest calling and purpose is to fulfill the spiritual and eternal kingdom of our Lord and Savior Jesus Christ. So first and foremost, we need to let the Church be the Church. Its goal is to exalt Christ—to preach, teach, and model the message of redemption is more important than anything else (see Matt. 28:18–20).

2. Pray.

So how do we let the Church be the Church? We pray. First Timothy 2:1–4 says, "I urge then, first of all, that petitions, prayers, intercession and thanksgiving be made for all people—for kings and all those in authority, that we may live peaceful and quiet lives in all godliness and holiness. This is good, and pleases God our Savior, who wants all people to be saved and to come to a knowledge of the truth."

We pray for those in authority, not so the economy gets better or to make our lives easier. We pray for our authorities so that there will be peace in the land. This in turn leads the way for the gospel to go forth so transformation can occur. This command holds true whether or not you agree with who is in power. The Scripture is clear: whoever is in office is ultimately established by God. And the first requirement of the Church and of individual believers is to pray for them.

Unfortunately, Christians have come to be characterized as narrow-minded, critical people who write, post pictures, blog, and email negative propaganda about those they oppose in elections. This is certainly not a fair assessment of most Christians, but the actions of some have painted Christians as hateful and unloving people. Despite their sincere motives and deep concerns over our moral decline, I fear our political profile has deeply undermined our primary focus—the gospel.

> **Unfortunately, Christians have come to be characterized as narrow-minded, critical people who write, post pictures, blog, and email negative propaganda about those they oppose in elections.**

I honestly wonder what would happen if we took a moment and prayed for the officials in authority. What if we cared about the souls of those in authority and truly, sincerely prayed for them to come to know the truth of Jesus Christ? What if we got to know them, took an interest in their lives, and tried to understand them before firing off the next email or petition?

3. Preach and teach.

After we pray as a church body, the Church is called to preach and teach the truth of God's Word. The Church is called to equip individual believers with a Biblical worldview. Teaching God's values helps individual Christians develop Biblical convictions about moral issues like abortion, sexuality, homosexuality, and stewardship of the environment. They have become "hot" and divisive issues in our day and Christians tend to align around their party affiliation (Democrat, Republican) instead of Scripture. God is looking for His children to choose His way first. He's looking for them to say, "God, I am Your child before I am a Democrat or a Republican or an Independent. What do You want me to do, what do You want me to say, and how do You want me to vote on these issues? Which candidates, regardless of party affiliation, will most honor You?" The Church's job is not to tell people how to vote but to teach what God declares as true.

Did you ever notice in John 18:37 that when Jesus was talking to Pilate He said, "Everyone on the side of truth listens to me"? Or when the Jewish leaders tried to trap Jesus, they said, "We know that you are a man of integrity and that you teach the way of God in accordance with the truth" (Matt. 22:16)?

So, is truth absolute or relative? If God's Word never changes, does truth? What is the truth about human sexuality? What is the truth about homosexuality? What is the truth about abortion and the environment? We are called to be the rudder of society by teaching and living the truth. That is the job of the Church.

4. Live the life.

In Acts 2:40–47 we see the early Church in action. The apostles prayed, devoted their time to preaching and teaching, and modeled a life devoted to Christ. People met at the temple for large group worship and instruction, and in homes, where they broke bread together. They lived in a decadent culture, with a corrupt government, where there was tremendous injustice, unspeakable immorality, and a god on every corner to worship. They were viewed as a radical sect or cult and accused of incest (because they called each other brother and sister) and were believed to be atheists (because they didn't worship the emperor as god).

Yet God empowered this small, countercultural group as they came together and walked and talked and acted like Jesus. They were politically powerless, but they surrendered their lives to Christ and met the deepest needs in their community. They didn't complain, they didn't gossip, they didn't judge. They cared. They fed the poor. They lived their lives together and loved one another. They changed the world. When the Church is the Church, we are our best, most influential selves. There's a role for individual believers in politics and the government must restrain evil, but transformation of the heart always precedes lasting transformation in the culture. How can that happen today?

Let's radically live out this model of spiritual integrity.

Start a ministry for unwed mothers, feed the poor, shelter the homeless, start a compassion ministry—just do something. When

Christians live like Christians, we are the most winsome, powerful group on the face of the earth!

So, let's live the life. Let's radically live out this model of spiritual integrity, the highest calling of Christ for the Church.

5. Don't expect the government to achieve what only the Church can do!

When political issues come up, I often hear fellow Christians say something like, "If we could only get the right person in office, we could turn this whole thing around and back to God." We unconsciously believe that the political process has the power to change the culture, change people's hearts, and make the world the way many Christians think it ought to be. But the Bible says the government has political limitations. Its ability solely rests in its power to restrain evil.

God says the foundations of His throne are justice and righteousness. He also says that righteousness exalts people and a nation. The government cannot create righteousness; only individual believers living out their faith in His power make that contribution.

I believe many Christians have unconsciously fallen into thinking moral and cultural change will come through some sort of messiah government group. With this thesis, we have witnessed thirty years of cultural wars, where the Church became a pawn in political power plays (by the left and the right). Each side believing that the "America we want" will be achieved when "we hold the White House, the majority in the Senate and the House, and appoint judges who think like us." Unfortunately, history has seen both the left and the right achieve the above with little or no change in violence, divorce, crime, poverty, and injustice. The government can't produce righteousness, but it can and does restrain evil.

Have you heard this before? "You can't legislate morality." And if by that, you mean you can't change people's hearts to have them do the right thing for the right reason, then I totally agree. Ironically, what laws actually are meant for is legislating morality. It's morally wrong to drive drunk—it puts you in jail. It is morally wrong to murder someone—it puts you in jail. It is morally wrong to steal or not pay your taxes—you get put in jail.

It's a personal relationship with Jesus Christ that changes you and changes the culture, from the inside out.

Those are moral issues. The government can legislate morality with laws that create boundaries to keep you protected. They can't bring about changes in the human heart. Our hope cannot be placed in candidates or political systems.

I love what Chuck Colson said: "The danger with Christian political movements, per se, is that they tend to make the gospel hostage to particular political agendas. You may wrap the cross in the flag and make God a prop for the state. And this is a grave danger."[1]

At the core of moral and cultural change is not changed laws, Supreme Court Justice appointments, or referendum victories. It's a personal relationship with Jesus Christ that changes you and changes the culture, from the inside out.

6. Don't expect the Church to accomplish what only individual believers can achieve!

As a pastor and church leader for over thirty years, I can tell you that a lot of people want the Church to promote their political agenda. I receive many letters and have multiple hallway conversations where I am strongly encouraged to "preach on that," interview candidates, take a stand, or pass out voting guides. What these Christians don't realize is that all those things are the role of the individual believer, not the Church. The overarching message of exalting Christ and the message of redemption and His kingdom agenda is God's priority when we're gathered corporately. God is not a Republican, Democrat, or Independent. He is absolutely 100 percent committed to having born-again, kingdom-minded followers fulfilling His agenda, above all others.

Unfortunately, the Church has been hijacked and the pulpit used by the Right and the Left to promote their agendas. God's Church has become a venue and vehicle to argue over issues, candidates, and agendas. Scriptural focus and kingdom principles are replaced with whom you should support and how you can help. At the end of the day, elections appear to tilt by the one the populous believes can make their lives and the economy better. When you get to the heart of it, far more than kingdom voters, we've become pragmatic materialists. We're not asking, "God, what do *You* want in this country? What do *You* want me to do?" We're asking, "Who has the better plan to make my life and my future better?" The Church and politics together has become a slippery slope, where much of what is said and done in the name of God is little more than idolatry, using God and His name to achieve personal agendas.

Scripture is very clear about our dual citizenship. We will be held accountable before God for our faithfulness in both arenas. The separatists and the activists both have it wrong. Separation for the Church is not the answer. Activism in the Church gathered is not the answer. The answer is two words: **individual responsibility!**

We have to ask ourselves, "If there is a kingdom of heaven that is spiritual and eternal and our allegiance is first to Christ, shouldn't that be our priority, first and foremost?" We all want the government to change things, we want the Church gathered to change things, but Jesus would say, "You are the light, you are the salt, you are the leaven."

> **Change comes when we as individuals see it is our responsibility—not the government's or the Church's—to make a difference.**

Change comes when we as individuals see it is our responsibility—not the government's or the Church's—to make a difference. Change happens when Christians begin to say, "I'm going to be informed. I'm going to vote. I'm going to find out the calling on my life to meet the real needs in my community." It's time to get out and actually do something that brings about real, concrete change in hurting people's lives. It's time to be Jesus to those who desperately need Him.

In his book *How Should Christians Vote?* Tony Evans has a chapter titled "Is God a Democrat or Republican?" And what he says is truly insightful about what our individual role in society should be.

Tony writes, "The Scripture clearly states the role of the believer, in the midst of society."[2]

He quotes Matthew 5:13–16: "You are the salt of the earth; but if the salt has become tasteless, how can it be made salty again? It is no longer good for anything, except to be thrown out and trampled under foot by men. You are the light of the world. A city set on a hill cannot be hidden, nor does anyone light a lamp and put it under a basket, but on the lampstand, and it gives light to all who are in the house. Let your light shine before men in such a way that they may see your good works, and glorify your Father who is in heaven" (NASB).

Tony continues, "Our job as Christians is to infiltrate where the bacteria of unrighteousness and darkness have permeated and made themselves at home. It's our job to act as salt and light in both parties and offer the Kingdom's point of view. One way you do that in a constitutional republic is through your vote."[3]

What is happening at the end of the day is that many of us want someone else to accomplish what God says is our job. So get informed, register to vote, and then actually vote. Of the sixty million evangelicals in the United States, only twenty million voted in the last election. That means two-thirds missed an opportunity to put God first and cast a kingdom vote.

The research I did on specific propositions, specific judges, and specific candidates showed that the win was accomplished by only a few hundred or a few thousand votes. Imagine if the other forty million evangelicals voted according to Biblical convictions, not party lines.

We've retreated and said, "The government solves the problems or gets the Church to be a political bully," rather than saying, "We're the salt, we're the light, we're the agents of change"—one person, one community at a time.

In some countries like Communist China, for example, you don't get to vote; you get to be a citizen. Yes, you get to live out your faith, but the moment they say you can't do something that God says you are supposed to do is when you'll exercise civil disobedience. You might be a Daniel and say, "I'm sorry, but you can't tell me that I cannot pray. I'm going to pray. Put me in jail, if that's the consequence; but I will still pray."

We are called to take part and participate under whatever government system we find ourselves. Some of you reading this book have a calling to be on a board of education or to lead a precinct of your political party. Perhaps you are going to be the next governor, mayor, or council member.

Before any of that can happen, however, you must be, above all else, known as a man, a woman, a student of God. It's a calling! God wants some of His children to serve Him in the political arena. He wants to change the institutions as His children walk humbly and winsomely in holiness. He wants to express His love through you, as you tactfully share what you believe and why you believe it. Let others observe your life and love even when you wholeheartedly disagree with their political perspective. God has worked and will work through committed followers of Jesus. Throughout history, Christians led the way in abolishing slavery, giving women the right to vote, supporting the Civil Rights Movement of the sixties, and now fighting the sex trafficking epidemic of our day.

Many will remember when the Berlin Wall fell, uniting Eastern and Western Germany. The wall fell, but the real story of what happened is a quiet story of believers empowered by Christ permeating the darkness, giving hope, meeting needs, and seeing God change the hearts and lives of the German people. A culture shift began and ended with the wall in rubble.

Can I tell you something? Your city doesn't have to stay the way it is. This country doesn't have to stay the way it is. The change can begin in your neighborhood, your kids, your school, and your community. The change starts with us. When we positively impact our culture by living like Jesus, like the early Church did, we will see God work in our "little world" in the same way.

In Conclusion

In a fallen world, God has a specific plan for transformation. The *Church* gathered is to teach and model truth whether or not that truth becomes the subject of political debate. The *government* is to pass and enforce laws to restrain evil. *Individual believers* are to take personal responsibility to exemplify Christ in the culture by life, word, and resources and engage in the political process as fully as the government allows.

When the roles of the Church, the government, and individual believers become clear and are applied faithfully, we diminish or eliminate a great majority of the conflict and division both inside and outside the Church. Godly Christians will not necessarily agree on non-moral and political issues, but we must take very seriously our citizenship in heaven, and our relationships with fellow Christians must override any of our strong and passionate political views. Unity in the body of Christ takes precedence over our personal political persuasions. Good people can "agree to disagree" with maturity.

For in the end, according to Jesus, they'll know us "by our love," not our political activity.

CHAPTER 8
WHERE DO WE GO FROM HERE?

Therefore everyone who hears these words of mine and puts them into practice is like a wise man who built his house on the rock. . . .

But everyone who hears these words of mine and does not put them into practice is like a foolish man who built his house on sand.

Matthew 7:24, 26
Jesus of Nazareth

We covered a lot of ground and tackled some tough issues in the preceding pages. Although they can be divisive and controversial, these five issues—human sexuality, homosexuality, abortion, the environment, and politics—are crucial to us as individual followers of Christ and the future of His Church. As unpopular as standing for truth (absolute truth) may be, it is vital to realize that these issues aren't new and God has something very important to say about each of them.

In fact, these issues are really only symptoms of a far deeper question in our day: What's the truth about Jesus, His Word, and His purpose for our lives?

So let's wrap up our discussion by examining truth in light of the life, claims, and teachings of Jesus.

What Does Jesus Say?

According to the Bible, Jesus lived a sinless life and rose from the dead. His life and teachings have always been powerful forces for cultural change and are to this very day. Slavery as a legal option was abolished on the basis of Christian principles; women came to be treated with respect and value because of Christian beliefs; and until the middle of the last century, ethics and law had been based primarily on the Judeo-Christian system of belief. So what did Jesus say

. . . About Himself?

Jesus made an outrageous claim about Himself in relation to truth. In fact, He claimed to *be* truth incarnate. The apostle John records that He told His followers, **"I am the way and the truth and the life. No one comes to the Father except through me"** (John 14:6).

Was Jesus intolerant? No, He was the most tolerant, loving, patient, accepting person to ever walk the face of the earth. He loved people unconditionally regardless of their sin, circumstances, or station in life. But when it came to truth He was equally straightforward. He stated that He was God and He held up His own life as the standard against which all others must be measured. "If you want to know what is right, what is true, how to live," He said, "look at Me."

Perhaps we've grown overly familiar with His statements. Perhaps they have lost their impact for our ears. In reality, Christ's claims were utterly scandalous! So ridiculous, in fact, that if He *hadn't* lived a perfect life, if He *hadn't* risen from the dead, His revolutionary message would be completely void.

However, if one takes the time to research the facts, the testimonies, and the historical documents, we learn that He did live a perfect life. He did rise from the dead. There is a powerful historical affirmation of those facts. Now, two thousand years later, people in every country of the world are still giving their lives to Him on the basis of that truth. Why? Because they have a personal relationship with Him and He is transforming them. He has forgiven their sin and provided answers to the deep metaphysical questions, the deep psychological questions, and the deepest spiritual issues of their lives. He has given them peace, brought change, granted forgiveness, and filled them with the joy of knowing God. That is what He claimed He would do.

. . . About His Word?

On the evening of the Last Supper, Jesus was preparing to go to the cross for your sins and mine. Facing the reality of His own imminent death, alone in the garden while His best friends slept, He began to talk to His Father about His greatest concern: you and me.

"Sanctify them by the truth; *your word is truth*," He prayed (John 17:17, emphasis added). To sanctify means to change, to set apart, to make holy. He wanted us to be made perfect, to reflect God's purity in our lives. And how was this miracle to take place? *By the Word of God*. God's objective standard for what is right, true, and moral, His framework for ethics and values, is presented to us in the inspired Scriptures, the Word of God.

Why Think?

So, where do *you* go from here? How will you discern between the relative message of our culture and the outrageous claims and historical proof of Jesus regarding truth?

I strongly encourage you to make it your goal to *think*. I mean *really* think. I wrote my master's thesis on the subject of absolute versus relative truth because I was struggling and didn't really know what I believed or why. I had a great experience with Jesus, but I had not done the hard work to address the nagging doubts and difficult questions I was facing in graduate school. I felt that if following God meant that I had to check my brains at the door, I couldn't follow Him with integrity. I was not willing to be a narrow-minded, Bible-thumping, "Well, God says it, so I believe it, that's it" kind of person. I couldn't base my life on dogma spoon-fed to me by someone else. My beliefs had to make sense and be intellectually feasible. They needed to have a basis in both fact and faith and handle the tough philosophical questions. And I had plenty of tough questions.

How do we account for both the particulars (each man's and each woman's unique design and value) and the universals that tie our existence together through time and history?

Where does personality come from?

How do I understand relationships in the context of life and culture?

And what about the issues of "being," of identity, about the possibility of the supernatural?

What Is the Purpose of My Life?

I felt that these issues had to be addressed. I was immature and arrogant and reasoned that if God had nothing to say about them in the Book He was supposed to have written, then I was simply shuffling through life, wasting my time on some "spiritual" pursuit.

But what I learned was that the more you ask of the Bible, the stronger the Bible answers back. I want to encourage you to consider looking into some of the books I've mentioned here (listed in the bibliography), to help you better understand how we arrived at the prevailing worldview embraced by many people today. But even more important, I encourage you to take your tough questions to the Bible. Make time in your schedule to dig into God's Word on a daily basis, and you will begin to see how far our world has digressed from the absolute truths you will find there.

The more you ask of the Bible, the stronger the Bible answers back.

God answers the questions of unity and diversity, and He speaks to the origin of personality. He explains why there's suffering and evil in the marred world, and He addresses the questions of free will and His sovereignty. And He does it all in the context of the culture of the day.

My hope is that you will take the time and effort to do your own research and **think things through for yourself** so that you are equipped to address the hard questions. Know what you believe and be able to defend it with love. Be ready to share the good news of Jesus Christ with your neighbor or your co-worker or your friend.

First Peter 3:15 reminds us to "Always be prepared to give an answer to everyone who asks you to give the reason for the hope that you have. But do this with gentleness and respect." As you search the Bible for answers, you will become more intimately acquainted with the God of this universe, who loved you enough to send His Son, who was willing to die for you, so that He might welcome you into His presence for all eternity.

So let's make a difference. Know your stuff. Get prepared and bring light not heat when these issues surface at work, at church, or around the Thanksgiving table with extended family. Silence is not an option! Arguments are fruitless. God has spoken, and we are His ambassadors to take the truth about human sexuality, homosexuality, abortion, the environment, and the Church and politics to a Church and world that desperately need it. We can share the truth in love, and the truth will set people free.

APPENDIX
Q&A ON HOMOSEXUALITY

Below are selected questions I have received, followed by my responses. All names are fictitious.

Question 1:

I just listened to part one of "Homosexuality Lifestyle." My niece in her mid-20s has been in this situation for about five years. She graduated from an all-girls' college and grew up in a liberal church with a lesbian minister. I decided not to attend her "marriage celebration" but did not tell her it was because I could not celebrate her lifestyle choice.

I felt like I had to choose between supporting family and being true to God. I would like to discuss this with her, but I fear losing a relationship with her and her parents. How do I decide what to do?

Nancy

Nancy, this question is one of the most common and difficult to answer. A number of variables are important to consider.

First, what kind of relationship do you have with your niece and her family? Is there significant history, depth, and an ongoing relationship; or is it casual, distant, and rare with regard to your personal interaction with them?

If it is the latter, your comments, no matter how sincere or well intended, will likely not be well received. There simply is not enough trust and relational capital for your perspective to be heard as both truthful and loving.

If, on the other hand, it's a fairly close relationship, then avoiding the issue creates awkwardness at best, and perceived judgment and disunity at worst.

With those two factors in view, you can prayerfully consider whether or not to speak with them. If God leads you to talk with them, let me provide the following short piece of advice.

Consider scheduling a time with her and her parents to express your concern and care for her as a person and, because of that love and concern, why you have struggled deeply with not attending her "marriage" ceremony. Express your desire to have an ongoing relationship and also your personal conflict. Explain to them that as a matter of personal integrity and your commitment to Jesus Christ, attending that celebration would communicate and condone what you believe is contrary to the will of God.

Allow them to see the depth of your personal struggle and the emotional turmoil that this situation has been for you in your heart. Let them know that you may disagree with her decision and lifestyle as a matter of principle, but that you very much care for her and her family and do not want to lose the relationship.

I think you will find this honest expression shared tenderly and from the heart will open the door for a relationship that can continue where you can keep your commitments to God and still love and provide a Christian witness for your niece and her family.

Question 2:

Recently, our 28-year-old son told us he is gay. We were completely blindsided by this revelation.

Now we have had to walk the journey of trying to maintain a relationship with him and to express our love even though he has pulled away from us—presumably due to our faith in Jesus Christ and what Scripture says about marriage.

My faith has been rocked, as it is so hard to understand how people of faith can have such polar opposite views about marriage and homosexuality. What is the truth?

I believe Jesus wants us to still love our son, but how do we speak the truth in love when we are confused by the mixed messages?

I look forward to hearing from you.

Bob

Bob, I recently had a good friend express exactly what you shared concerning your son. The word "blindsided" is an apt description. First and foremost, know you are not alone, and getting strong personal support around you is critical right now. Our initial responses when blindsided are often not the wisest or the most productive. Get wise, Biblical counsel to help you navigate with both truth and love.

Since I already discussed how to frame the issue and develop a plan that honors differences but is committed to a real relationship (see question 1), let me address the second part of your question, "How can people of faith have such polar opposite views on marriage and homosexuality?" I'm going to refer you to two web articles and a book that I believe address this issue fairly and with intellectual and academic substance and integrity. The first article, by Dr. Ken Boa (MIT grad, PhDs from Dallas Seminary and Oxford), a good friend and brilliant thinker, addresses this issue graciously in "Homosexuality and the Meaning of Love." The second is by Dr. Daniel Wallace, who answers Mel White (a former associate of Billy Graham who has come out as gay in recent years and makes what he believes to be a Biblical case for monogamous homosexual relationships). For those from more conservative Biblically oriented churches, this is a growing position among some young evangelicals and has been the position of mainline denominations that approve of gay marriage and clergy. (See the bibliography for web addresses.) These articles are relatively short, explain the issues without too much technical language, and are written compassionately to communicate the truth, not attack people.

The third resource is a book entitled *Homosexuality and the Bible: Two Views* by Dan O. Via and Robert A. J. Gagnon. This is a longer and more in-depth analysis that covers every major text in the Bible on homosexuality. The men take opposing positions on the topic, but do so in a spirit of grace and understanding.

The first author, Dr. Via, is honest in clearly communicating that he does not view Scripture as it was historically written as authoritative or without error. His position essentially modifies what Scripture states based on what he considers information and cultural developments unavailable to the apostle Paul. His conclusion is that homosexuality is an acceptable lifestyle for Christians in monogamous homosexual relationships.

The second author, Dr. Gagnon, does careful exegesis of every Biblical passage pertaining to the topic. He explains the historical, cultural, and grammatical issues related to each text and concludes that homosexual acts are forbidden by God as sexually immoral practices in the same manner that adultery and fornication are forbidden heterosexual practices.

It is absolutely essential in our day to become educated on how homosexuality is being redefined among Christians and realize that for those who hold Scripture as God's Word and the authoritative guide for faith and practice, the core issue will not be homosexuality but hermeneutics. What's at stake is Scripture itself. There is an emerging approach to interpreting God's Word (even among evangelicals) in a way that removes moral absolutes.

Question 3:

My name is Jane. I have a daughter who is in a lesbian relationship. She has spoken to me about it and knows it is wrong but feels that this is what she is going to do right now. She has had sexual abuse in her childhood, which I just found out about last year. Her dad struggled with drug addiction all her life. She is 20 years old. I just feel so bad for her.

233

I know she is searching and wants to find love. She is a believer and I believe she is going to come out of this, but it is a struggle. I wanted to know if you have any resources, and please pray for me. I know you had a sermon on this awhile back. I don't want to condone this behavior, but I want to show her love.

Yes, Jane, we do have resources that can help you personally on this journey and to learn how to communicate both truth and love to your daughter.

This teaching on homosexuality in chapter 4 is a great place to begin. Also, you will notice endnotes and a bibliography that, by their titles, can help you address a wide variety of related issues.

Finally, we have discovered that the support of others and a place to process your journey is critical to empower you to respond with both truth and love. Often, the best wisdom from God comes from those who know you and your daughter the best as you study God's Word together. This entire *Culture Shock* series is available from livingontheedge.org in a small group DVD format with study guides that will help you explore and apply this teaching.

Question 4:

My son is 38 and gay . . . and we had a wonderful relationship. I have known for so long he was gay. My pain of course is that, but also why the church will not allow gays to join. Please explain to me; my son-in-law is my pastor and it really hurts.

I feel the church is talking with a forked tongue . . . saying one thing and doing another. So right now my son is a member nowhere; he doesn't have to be a member, but I would love for him to be. Tell me your reasons behind why he can't join the church since our God says one sin is no bigger.

Thank you in advance for addressing this issue.

Gloria

Gloria, God loves all people. Jesus died to forgive the sins of the whole world (John 3:16). Whoever repents from their sin and receives the free gift of eternal life by faith in Jesus Christ becomes a part of His Family—the body of Christ.

Local churches are expressions of the universal body of Christ (all believers who have trusted Christ personally and in whom His Spirit now dwells). Jesus commanded His disciples, then and now, to come out from the world and live pure and holy lives (see the Sermon on the Mount in Matthew chapters 5–8, and Romans 12:2). The early apostles all taught that our salvation is by God's free gift of grace and that this grace leads to a holy life characterized by sexual purity (Titus 2:11–14). Adultery, fornication, and homosexuality were all common practices in Jesus's day and in the early Church. The new spiritual birth of salvation brings with it new life and a new lifestyle. Read the following New Testament passages to see this pattern:

But just as he who called you is holy, so be holy in all you do; for it is written: "Be holy, because I am holy." (1 Peter 1:15–16)

But among you there must not be even a hint of sexual immorality, or of any kind of impurity, or of greed, because these are improper for God's holy people. Nor should there be obscenity, foolish talk or coarse joking, which are out of place, but rather thanksgiving. For of this you can be sure: No immoral, impure or greedy person—such a person is an idolater—has any inheritance in the kingdom of Christ and of God. Let no one deceive you with empty words, for because of such things God's wrath comes on those who are disobedient. Therefore do not be partners with them. For you were once darkness, but now you are light in the Lord. Live as children of light (for the fruit of the light consists in all goodness, righteousness and truth). (Eph. 5:3–9)

We know that we have come to know him if we keep his commands. Whoever says, "I know him," but does not do what he commands is a liar, and the truth is not in that person. But if anyone obeys his word, love for God is truly made complete in them. This is how we know we are in him: Whoever claims to live in him must live as Jesus did. (1 John 2:3–6)

Gloria, as followers of Jesus we all fail and still sin on occasion, but it's not the desire of our heart or the habitual pattern of our lives. But the Bible is very clear that to continue willfully in known sin is not an option for a genuine follower of Jesus. This is true for all sins, not just homosexuality. Someone having an affair, living with someone but not married, habitually lying or gossiping, all forfeit the privileges of active membership in a local body of Christ. In 1 Corinthians 5:9–13, the early Church was commanded to not associate with those who claimed to be Christians but who willfully continued in sexual immorality of whatever kind.

Unfortunately, the Church has been selective at times in its application and obedience to this command. Churches have tended to point out certain sexual sins (like homosexuality) and overlooked other habitual sins (like gossip and gluttony). This passage, however, applies to all people, not simply people living in disobedience in their sexual lives, whether that be homosexuality, adultery, or fornication.

Your son is welcome to enjoy the fellowship and membership of a local church if he chooses to repent of his sexual sin. If, however, he chooses to continue in his present lifestyle, your son-in-law, who is your pastor, is seeking to obey God's Word and protect the reputation and purity of the bride of Christ—the Church—by not allowing your son membership.

Question 5:

My oldest daughter, who has married another woman, called to tell me that they are now expecting a baby. Her partner has been artificially inseminated and is 6 months pregnant. I know she was hoping I'd be excited but also knew that I didn't approve. I tried to tell her graciously how I felt about this, and I know she could tell from my voice that I wasn't excited. I just don't know how to respond to this. I feel so bad for her because her siblings all are married and have children, and I've been excited for each of them, but for this daughter I am not. When I said something, she responded, "I knew you'd criticize me and put me down." I admit during her growing-up years, I did criticize a lot and had a hard time finding things to compliment her on, and for this, I feel responsible for her homosexuality. Our relationship was not very good. I see in retrospect how differently I could have handled situations with her and loved her through all the difficulties we had. But now, I just feel so bad that with the decisions she has made, I don't agree. I just don't know what to say to her. She moved to the other side of the country and now there will be an innocent child that I will be a grandmother to, although long distance.

Like I said, I just don't know how to respond to her. I know what truth is, and how God wants our families to be. I don't approve of her lifestyle, but I love my daughter.

Thank you for any advice you can give.

Lori

Lori, your letter has a number of issues interwoven within it. I hear your heartbreak and concern for your daughter, your guilt concerning your past treatment of your daughter, and some important questions about the future. Let's take them one at a time.

First, although none of us are perfect parents, when we know we've made specific mistakes, we need to own those personally and ask God for forgiveness (1 John 1:9). I encourage you to find some uninterrupted time alone and ask God to show you the specific ways you have not loved your daughter in the past and the things you believe you did that were wrong. Then I encourage you to bring those specific acts and attitudes before God the Father and ask for His forgiveness based on Jesus's work on the cross.

Second, you need to communicate to your daughter, totally apart from her lifestyle issues, your sincere regret for your past actions and ask for her forgiveness. It will be important to be specific and share some specific times or instances that you most regret where possible. A face-to-face is always hardest, but best; but if that is not possible, a handwritten letter that owns your failure and sin, expresses the depth of your sorrow and regret, and asks for her forgiveness is another powerful option. Let her know you want to rebuild the relationship as a mother and daughter.

Next, be gentle but forthright about her lesbian lifestyle and her decision to marry a woman and have a baby with her partner. Express that you understand her deep desire as a woman for a loving relationship and to be a mother. Those desires are legitimate and God-given, but His design is for these to be fulfilled with a man. Let her know you love her and you want to be a part of her life as much as possible, but that she needs to own the implications and consequences of her decisions and actions just as you have done. You deeply love her, but can't condone or agree with her choices or lifestyle.

Admit that your lack of excitement is because you are torn and conflicted personally. Help her understand, as best you can, how painful and difficult it is for you because you want to affirm her as a person, yet can't accept her behavior and choices that are in direct contradiction with the clear teaching of Jesus and Scripture.

She has the freedom to choose to live in whatever kind of sexual lifestyle she chooses, but she must also realize that her choices have placed you in a difficult position. As kindly as possible, you want to communicate that she needs to accept that, as much as you want a relationship with her and as sorry as you are for past mistakes, for you to condone her lifestyle and celebrate those choices would cause you to compromise your obedience to Christ and His word.

The final step is to agree that your love for her and commitment to her doesn't change, but the expectations and ways in which to express that love will have boundaries and limits based on her choices. Let her know you want to talk with her and explore together what it looks like in your particular relationship (and family dynamics) to express love, have regular interaction, and build a relationship in a way that you honor her choices (which you disagree with) and she honors your Biblical convictions (that she disagrees with).

As I talk with Christian parents, there is a tendency to allow the son or daughter who has "come out" to frame the conversation and set the new paradigm. In other words, the person "coming out" says, "This is how I'm going to live (based on the false premise that it's who I am); therefore, if you don't accept my decisions and actions to live a homosexual lifestyle and continue to enjoy all the family relationships and privileges as before, then you as a Christian are unloving and, therefore, a hypocrite."

It's critical in these initial conversations to set aside the emotion, grief, and fear that this moment involves and clearly frame the relationship moving forward in light of "who moved." You want to communicate your willingness to respect and honor their right to make lifestyle choices, but remind them that with those choices come implications and consequences. Just as they want you to honor their lifestyle and convictions about their sexuality, so they must understand they must honor your lifestyle and convictions as a follower of Jesus Christ.

Having dealt with this issue numerous times, I know the temptation is to avoid this difficult **Truth in Love** approach. The Truth Only approach is often characterized by emotional outbursts and anger and cuts the person out of their lives, stops any interaction or communication, and reinforces the "bigoted Christian" stereotypes. The Love Only approach refuses to face the issue honestly and Biblically and hopes things will change someday. Family members passively act as though nothing really has changed. The lack of honest, loving confrontation communicates that family members condone the lifestyle and the sinful behavior publicly while often living in angst privately.

To ask your question or leave a comment,
log on to cultureshockthebook.com.

We look forward to hearing from you,

Chip

NOTES

Chapter 1 Whatever Happened to Right and Wrong?

1. Josh McDowell and Bob Hostetler, *Right from Wrong* (Nashville: Word Publishing, 1994), 3–4.

2. Ibid., 6.

Chapter 2 How Did We Get into This Mess?

1. The excerpts from this subsection, A Snapshot from a Local High School Student, are taken from "God," Santa Cruz High School newspaper, September 1996.

2. Barna Group, "Barna Survey Examines Changes in Worldview Among Christians over the Past 13 Years," Barna.org, March 26, 2009, https://www.barna.org/barna-update/21-transformation/252-barna-survey-examines-changes-in-worldview-among-christians-over-the-past-13-years#.Uv5fWMko6cx.

3. Ibid.; see also George Barna and Mark Hatch, *Boiling Point* (Ventura, CA: Regal Books, 2001).

4. Barna and Hatch, *Boiling Point*, 202.

Chapter 3 Human Sexuality

1. Save America Ministries, "Sexual Seduction of the Union: A Sexual Portrait of American Life," July 1, 2003, http://saveus.org/fact-sheets-articles/; Alan Petigny and Cathy Keen, "Silent Sexual Revolution Began in 1940s and '50s," *Explore*, 10, no. 1 (Spring 2005), http://www.research.ufl.edu/publications/explore/v10n1/extract4.html; Heather Boonstra, "Teen Pregnancy: Trends and Lessons Learned," *The Guttmacher Report on Public Policy* 5, no. 1 (February 2002), http://www.guttmacher.org/pubs/tgr/05/1/gr050107.html; "Premarital Sex," http://www.faculty.fairfield.edu/faculty/hodgson/Courses/so142/premarital/premaritalTs.htm, excerpted from "Teenagers in the United States: Sexual Activity, Contraceptive Use, and Childbearing, 2002," CDC Vital and Health Statistics, series 23, no. 24 (December 2004).

2. See Marvin Olasky, "Strange Bedfellows," *WORLD*, July 14, 2012, 9–11.

3. Walt and Barb Larimore, *His Brain, Her Brain* (Grand Rapids: Zondervan, 2008), 52.

4. Robert Moeller, "Sex in America: Good News and Bad News," *Current Thoughts and Trends* 12, no. 2 (February 1996): item 10836.

5. Ibid.

6. Michael Foust, "'Living Together' Before Marriage a Statistical Risk," Fireproof-MyMarriage.com, http://www.google.com/url?sa=t&rct=j&q=&esrc=s&source=web&cd=5&ved=0CFUQFjAE&url=http%3A%2F%2Fwww.fireproofmymarriage.com%2Fdload.php%3Ffile%3D_images%2F_couples%2FLivingtogetherStatistical Risk.pdf&ei=DVz6Uq37JsXs2QWS2oB4&usg=AFQjCNFZSmPnR05La8-0BDBU9f Gf8DnRKQ&bvm=bv.61190604,d.b2I.

7. Bruce Marshall, *The World, The Flesh, and Father Smith* (Boston: Houghton Mifflin, 1945), 108.

Chapter 4 Homosexuality

1. David Moore, *Five Lies of the Century* (Carol Stream, IL: Tyndale, 1995), 224.

2. "Homosexuality: Born or Bred?" *Newsweek*, February 23, 1992 (updated March 3, 2010), http://www.newsweek.com/homosexuality-born-or-bred-200636. For more on the science and popular handling of the research, see Moore, *Five Lies of the Century*, 227.

3. "Homosexuality: Born or Bred?"

4. Ibid.

5. Moore, *Five Lies of the Century*, 226.

6. Joseph Nicolosi, PhD, *Reparative Therapy of Male Homosexuality* (Northvale, NJ: Jason Aronson, Inc., 1991), 25.

7. See S. Doll et al., "Self-Reported Childhood and Adolescent Sexual Abuse Among Adult Homosexual Bisexual Men," *Child Abuse and Neglect* 16, no. 6 (1992): 855–64.

8. Margaret L. Usdonsky, "Gay Couples, by the Numbers," *USA Today*, April 12, 1993, 8A.

9. Philip Elmer-DeWitt, "Now the Truth About Americans and Sex," *Time*, October 17, 1994, 68.

10. H. H. Hartfield, "Sexually Transmitted Diseases in Homosexual Men," 1981.

11. *Washington Blade*, October 9, 1998, as cited in Karen Testerman, "Promiscuous Plague," WorldandI.com, March 2004, http://www.worldandi.com/newhome/public/2004/March/cipub1print.asp.

12. Testerman, "Promiscuous Plague."

13. National Center for Infectious Diseases, 1992, as cited in ibid.

14. "Sex Survey Results," *Genre* (October 1996), quoted in "Survey Finds 40 Percent of Gay Men Have Had More Than 40 Sex Partners," *Lambda Report*, January 1998: 20.

15. Paul Van de Ven et al., "A Comparative Demographic and Sexual Profile of Older Homosexually Active Men," *Journal of Sex Research* 34 (1997): 354.

16. Richard B. Hays, *The Moral Vision of the New Testament* (San Francisco: Harper One, 1996), 381.

17. Mark Schwarta and William Masters, "The Masters and Johnson Treatment Program for Dissatisfied Homosexual Men," *American Journal of Psychiatry* (February 1984): 173–81.

18. Ibid.

Chapter 5 Abortion

1. Guttmacher Institute, "Facts on Induced Abortion in the United States," August 2011, http://www.guttmacher.org/pubs/fb_induced_abortion.pdf, updated 2014 Fact Sheet.

2. Literature referred to includes documents from Planned Parenthood, the California Abortion and Reproductive Rights Action League (CARAL), The Alan Guttmacher Institute, and Centers for Disease Control (CDC).

3. National Right to Life literature, http://www.nrlc.org/about/.

4. Document from Planned Parenthood, 1996.

5. Real Options data, Pregnancy Medical Clinics, RealOptions.net.

6. "Thinking about Abortion," PlannedParenthood.org, http://m.plannedparenthood.org/mt/www.plannedparenthood.org/health-topics/pregnancy/thinking-about-abortion-21519.htm?un_jtt_v_expand=1.

7. Guttmacher Institute, "Facts on Induced Abortion in the United States."

8. Randy O'Bannon, "56,662,169 Abortions in America Since Roe vs. Wade in 1973," LifeNews.com, January 12, 2014, http://www.lifenews.com/2014/01/12/56662169-abortions-in-america-since-roe-vs-wade-in-1973/.

9. Serrin Foster, "The Feminist Case *Against* Abortion," Feminists for Life, reprinted by permission from *The Commonwealth*, Sept. 13, 1999, at http://feministsforlife.org/-news/commonw.htm.

10. A more complete analysis of abortion history can be found in Tim Stafford, "The Abortion Wars: What Most Christians Don't Know," *Christianity Today*, October 1989, 16–20.

11. "The Legal Status of Abortion in America," Christian Action Council, 1995.

12. Melody Green, "Children, Things We Throw Away?" Last Days Ministries, 1986. http://www.lastdaysministries.org/Articles/1000008517/Last_Days_Ministries/LDM/Discipleship_Teachings/Melody_Green/Children_Things_We.aspx.

13. Guttmacher Institute 2008.

14. O'Bannon, "56,662,169 Abortions."

15. "Fetal Development," MedlinePlus, http://www.nlm.nih.gov/medlineplus/ency/article/002398.htm; "What Your Baby Looks Like This Week," babycenter.com, http://www.babycenter.com/fetal-development-week-by-week; "Fetal Development," pregnancy.org, http://www.pregnancy.org/fetaldevelopment.

16. "The Legal Status of Abortion in America," Christian Action Council, 1995.

17. Elizabeth Cornwell, as cited in Kristine Kruszelnicki, "Pro-Life Advocates Take Message to Atheist Convention," LifeNews.com, March 29, 2012, http://www.lifenews.com/2012/03/29/pro-life-advocates-take-message-to-atheist-convention/.

18. Christopher Hitchens, as cited in Kruszelnicki, "Pro-Life Advocates."

19. Frank E. Gabelein, gen. ed., *The Expositor's Bible Commentary*, vol. 2 (Grand Rapids: Zondervan, 1992), 434–35.

Chapter 6 The Environment

1. L. E. Holt and R. McIntosh, *Holt Pediatrics,* 12th ed. (New York: Appleton-Century-Crofts, 1953), 125–26.

Chapter 7 Politics

1. Chuck Colson, cited in "The Christian as Citizen: Three Views," *Christianity Today*, vol. 29, 1985, 24.

2. Tony Evans, *How Should Christians Vote?* (Chicago: Moody, 2012), 78.

3. Ibid.

BIBLIOGRAPHY

"An Introduction to Climate Change: What It Could Mean to You and Your Family." NRDC. org, revised November 8, 2011. http://www.nrdc.org/globalwarming/climatebasics.asp.

Anderson, Kerby. "Homosexual Theology." Bible.org, May 30, 2008. http://bible.org/article/homosexual-theology.

Barna Group. "A New Generation of Adults Bends Moral and Sexual Rules to Their Liking." Barna.org, October 31, 2006. https://www.barna.org/barna-update/article/13-culture/144-a-new-generation-of-adults-bends-moral-and-sexual-rules-to-their-liking#.UwN7w7Su5No.

Barna Group. "Barna Survey Examines Changes in Worldview Among Christians over the Past 13 Years." Barna.org, March 26, 2009. https://www.barna.org/barna-update/21-transformation/252-barna-survey-examines-changes-in-worldview-among-christians-over-the-past-13-years#.Uv5fWMko6cx.

Barna, George, and Mark Hatch. *Boiling Point*. Ventura, CA: Regal Books, 2001.

Belz, Joel. "Fine-Tuning the Nuances: The Difference Between the Church Gathered and the Church Dispersed." *WORLD*, June 8, 2002. http://www.worldmag.com/2002/06/fine_tuning_the_nuances.

Boa, Kenneth. "All That Heaven Allows: Homosexuality and the Meaning of Love." Bible. org, March 27, 2006. https://bible.org/seriespage/all-heaven-allows-homosexuality-and-meaning-love.

Bohlin, Sue. "Answers to Questions Most Asked by Gay-Identifying Youth." Bible.org, September 28, 2009. http://bible.org/article/answers-questions-most-asked-gay-identifying-youth.

Boonstra, Heather. "Teen Pregnancy: Trends and Lessons Learned." *The Guttmacher Report on Public Policy* 5, no. 1 (February 2002). http://www.guttmacher.org/pubs/tgr/05/1/gr050107.html.

Cable, Stephen. *Cultural Captives: The Beliefs and Behavior of American Young Adults*. Plano, TX: Probe Ministries, 2013.

"The Christian as Citizen: Three Views." *Christianity Today* 29 (1985): 24–27.

"Cohabiting Couples Have Lower Premarital Satisfaction." *Prepare/Enrich Newsletter* 2, no. 2 (Fall 1988).

Dallas, Joe. "Born Gay? How Politics Have Skewed the Debate over the Biological Causes of Homosexuality." *Christianity Today,* June 22, 1992, 20–23, 29.

Doll, S., et al. "Self-Reported Childhood and Adolescent Sexual Abuse Among Adult Homosexual Bisexual Men." *Child Abuse and Neglect* 16, no. 6 (1992): 855–64.

Elmer-Dewitt, Philip. "Now for the Truth about Americans and Sex." *Time,* October 17, 1994, 64.

Evans, Tony. *How Should Christians Vote?* Chicago: Moody Publishers, 2012.

"Fetal Development," MedlinePlus, http://www.nlm.nih.gov/medlineplus/ency/article/002398.htm.

"Fetal Development," Pregnancy.org, http://www.pregnancy.org/fetaldevelopment.

Foust, Michael. "'Living Together' Before Marriage a Statistical Risk." Fireproofmy Marriage.com. http://www.google.com/url?sa=t&rct=j&q=&esrc=s&sourc e=web&cd=5&ved=0CFUQFjAE&url=http%3A%2F%2Fwww.fireproofmy marriage.com%2Fdload.php%3Ffile%3D_images%2F_couples%2FLivingtoget herStatisticalRisk.pdf&ei=DVz6Uq37JsXs2QWS2oB4&usg=AFQjCNFZSmPn R05La8-0BDBU9fGf8DnRKQ&bvm=bv.61190604,d.b2I.

Fowler, Richard A., and H. Wayne House. *The Christian Confronts His Culture.* Part Three: The Homosexuality Issue. Chicago: Moody, 1983. 117–29.

Gabelein, Frank E., gen. ed. *The Expositor's Bible Commentary.* Vol. 2. Grand Rapids: Zondervan, 1992.

Gomez, Mark. "Can Christians Be Faithful and Political? 7 Critical Issues." ChurchLeaders .com. http://www.churchleaders.com/pastors/pastor-articles/161202-mark_ gomez_faithful_and_political_7_critical_issues_for_engaging_politics.html?p=1.

Green, Melody. "Children, Things We Throw Away?" Last Days Ministries, 1986. http://www.lastdaysministries.org/Articles/1000008517/Last_Days_Ministries/ LDM/Discipleship_Teachings/Melody_Green/Children_Things_We.aspx.

Guttmacher Institute. "Facts Sheet: Induced Abortion in the United States." Guttmacher.org.

Hays, Richard B. Part Four: The Pragmatic Task. In *The Moral Vision of the New Testament: A Contemporary Introduction to New Testament Ethics.* San Francisco: Harper One, 1996. See esp. chap. 16, "Homosexuality."

Holt, L. E., and R. McIntosh (1953). *Holt Pediatrics,* 12th ed. (New York: Appleton-Century-Crofts, 1953.

"Homosexuality: Born or Bred?" *Newsweek,* February 23, 1992. http://www.newsweek.com/homosexuality-born-or-bred-200636.

Homosexuals in the Church. Christianity Today Bible Study. ChristianBibleStudies. com. http://www.christianitytoday.com/biblestudies/.

Jackson, Wayne. "A Critical Look at Situation Ethics." ChristianCourier.com, updated: Friday, August 31, 2001. http://www.christiancourier.com/feature/march99.htm.

"Josh McDowell's personal notes on Teen Statistics." The Last Christian Generation? Fourpercent.blogspot.com, September 13, 2009. http://fourpercent.blogspot. com/2009/09/josh-mcdowells-personal-notes-on-teen.html.

Kruszelnicki, Kristine. "Pro-Life Advocates Take Message to Atheist Convention." LifeNews.com, March 29, 2012. http://www.lifenews.com/2012/03/29/ pro-life-advocates-take-message-to-atheist-convention/.

Kumar, Anugrah. "Apologist Josh McDowell: Internet the Greatest Threat to Christians." ChristianPost.com, July 16, 2011. http://www.christianpost.com/news/internet-the-greatest-threat-to-christians-apologist-josh-mcdowell-says-52382/.

Larimore, Walt, and Barb Larimore. *His Brain, Her Brain.* Grand Rapids: Zondervan, 2008.

LeVay, Simon. "A Difference in Hypothalamic Structure between Heterosexual and Homosexual Men," *Science* 258 (1991): 1034–7.

Marshall, Bruce. *The World, The Flesh, and Father Smith.* Boston: Houghton Mifflin, 1945.

McDowell, Josh, and Bob Hostetler. *Right from Wrong.* Nashville: Word Publishing, 1994.

Miller, Lisa. "Beliefwatch: Pro-Life Atheists," Newsweek.com, November 28, 2008 (updated March 13, 2010). http://www.newsweek.com/beliefwatch-pro-life-atheists-85273.

Moeller, Robert. "Sex in America: Good News and Bad News." *Current Thoughts and Trends* 12, no. 2 (February 1996): item 10836.

Moore, David. "Sex from the Inventor's Point of View." Chap. 12 in *Five Lies of the Century.* Carol Stream, IL: Tyndale, 1995.

Morrison, Todd. "Can I Come to Your Church? I'm Gay." *Relevant*, May 24, 2012. http://www.relevantmagazine.com/god/church/blog/29292-qcan-i-come-to-your-church-im-gayq.

National Right to Life. http://www.nrlc.org/.

Natural Resources Defense Council. www.nrdc.org/issues: conserving wild fisheries, energy, environment and health, global warming, oceans, sustainable communities, water, wildlife.

Nicolosi, Joseph. *Reparative Therapy of Male Homosexuality.* Northvale, NJ: Jason Aronson, Inc., 1991.

O'Bannon, Randy. "56,662,169 Abortions in America Since Roe vs. Wade in 1973." LifeNews.com, January 12, 2014. http://www.lifenews.com/2014/01/12/56662169-abortions-in-america-since-roe-vs-wade-in-1973/.

Olasky, Marvin. "Strange Bedfellows." *WORLD*, July 14, 2012, 9–11.

Petigny, Alan, and Cathy Keen. "'Silent' Sexual Revolution Began in 1940s and '50s." *Explore*, 10, no. 1 (Spring 2005). http://www.research.ufl.edu/publications/explore/v10n1/extract4.html.

Planned Parenthood. "Thinking About Abortion." PlannedParenthood.org, http://m.plannedparenthood.org/mt/www.plannedparenthood.org/health-topics/pregnancy/thinking-about-abortion-21519.htm?un_jtt_v_expand=1.

"Premarital Sex." http://www.faculty.fairfield.edu/faculty/hodgson/Courses/so142/premarital/premaritalTs.htm.

Save America Ministries. "Sexual Seduction of the Union: A Sexual Portrait of American Life." July 1, 2003. http://saveus.org/fact-sheets-articles/.

Schrof, Joanie M., and Betsy Wagner. "Sex in America," *U.S. News & World Report*, October 17, 1994, 77.

Schwarta, Mark, and William Masters. "The Masters and Johnson Treatment Program for Dissatisfied Homosexual Men." *American Journal of Psychiatry* (February 1984): 173–81.

"Sex Survey Results." *Genre*, October 1996. Quoted in "Survey Finds 40 Percent of Gay Men Have Had More Than 40 Sex Partners." *Lambda Report*, January 1998: 20.

Sherman, Dean. "Singles & Sex: Logical, Loving Limits." Last Days Ministries, March 26, 2012. http://www.lastdaysministries.org/Groups/1000087866/Last_Days_Ministries/Articles/Other_Authors/Singles_Sex/Singles_Sex.aspx.

Slick, Matt. "Christianity and Homosexuality." Christian Apologetics & Research Ministry. http://carm.org/christianity-and-homosexuality.

Stafford, Tim. "The Abortion Wars, What Most Christians Don't Know." *Christianity Today*, October 1989, 16–20. Reprinted January 1, 2003. http://www.christianity today.com/ct/2003/januaryweb-only/1-20-31.0.html.

Stone, Dave. "Same-Sex Attraction." Trending series, LW 3664, June 30, 2013. Southeast Christian Church, Louisville, KY. http://www.southeastchristian.org/default.aspx?page=4754&series=54.

Stott, John. *Volume 1 Involvement: Being a Responsible Christian in a Non-Christian Society*. Old Tappan, NJ: Fleming H. Revell, 1985. See esp. chap. 1, "Involvement: Is It Our Concern?"; and chap. 6, "Our Human Environment."

Strauss, Lehman. "Homosexuality: The Christian Perspective." Angelfire.com. http://www.angelfire.com/al4/cornerstone/pervertedlifestyle.html.

Testerman, Karen. "Promiscuous Plague." WorldandI.com, March 2004, http://www.worldandi.com/newhome/public/2004/March/cipub1print.asp.

"The Shift from Smut to Big Business!" *U.S. News & World Report*, 1997.

Usdonsky, Margaret L. "Gay Couples, by the Numbers." *USA Today*, April 12, 1993, 8A.

Van de Ven, Paul, et al. "A Comparative Demographic and Sexual Profile of Older Homosexually Active Men." *Journal of Sex Research* 34 (1997): 354.

Via, Dan O., and Robert A.J. Gagnon. *Homosexuality and the Bible: Two Views*. Minneapolis: Fortress Press, 2009.

Wallace, Daniel B. "Review of Mel White's 'What the Bible Says—and Doesn't Say—about Homosexuality.'" Bible.org, November 6, 2006. https://bible.org/article/review-mel-white-s-what-bible-says-and-doesn-t-say-about-homosexuality.

"What Your Baby Looks Like This Week," babycenter.com, http://www.babycenter.com/fetal-development-week-by-week.

White, James R., and Jeffrey D. Niell. *The Same-Sex Controversy: Defending and Clarifying the Bible's Message About Homosexuality*. Minneapolis: Bethany House, 2002.

Wikipedia. S.v. "Great Pacific Garbage Patch." http://en.wikipedia.org/wiki/Great_Pacific_Garbage_Patch.

Chip Ingram is the teaching pastor for Living on the Edge, an international teaching and discipleship ministry, and senior pastor of Venture Christian Church in Los Gatos, California. His passion is to help everyday Christians actually "live like Christians" by raising the bar of discipleship. A pastor for over twenty years, Chip has a unique ability to communicate truth and winsomely challenge people to live out their faith. Chip is the author of thirteen books, including *Finding God When You Need Him Most*; *True Spirituality: Becoming a Romans 12 Christian*; *Good to Great in God's Eyes*; and *God: As He Longs for You to See Him*. Chip and his wife, Theresa, have four children and nine grandchildren. For more information about Chip Ingram, please visit www.LivingOnTheEdge.org.

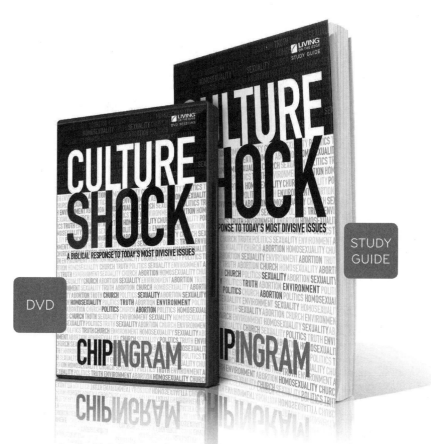

ALSO AVAILABLE

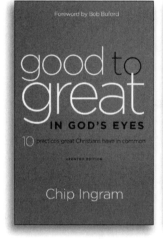

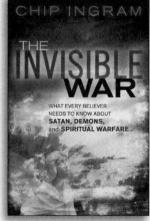

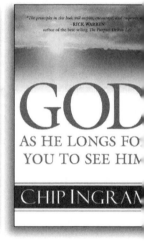

"This book will redirect, empower, and inspire you on your own journey to greatness."

—**Gregg Dedrick**, former president, KFC

The Invisible War is a balanced and Biblically informed book that examines what every believer needs to know about Satan, demons, and spiritual warfare.

God: As He Longs for You to See Him is an accessibl but challenging look at the attributes of God and show that our view of God impac every decision in our lives

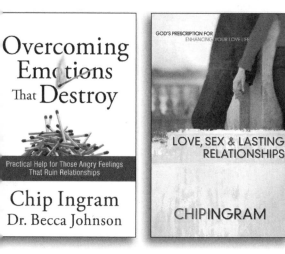